THE BIRTH OF SEATTLE RAP

THE BIRTH OF

SEATTLE RAP

NOVOCAINE132

Foreword by DJ Nasty-Nes

Published by The History Press
Charleston, SC
www.historypress.com

First published 2025

Manufactured in the United States

ISBN 9781467158244

Library of Congress Control Number: 2024947365

Notice: The information in this book is true and complete to the best of our knowledge. It is offered without guarantee on the part of the author or The History Press. The author and The History Press disclaim all liability in connection with the use of this book.

CONTENTS

Foreword, by DJ Nasty-Nes 7
Acknowledgements 9
Introduction 11

1980
Disco Breaks 13
DJ Nasty-Nes and Sheila Locke 18
Terrible Two 20

1981
Jam Delight 23
Cosmic Crew 25
"I'm Little Ray Rapper" 27
Sir Mix-A-Lot 31
SNECO 32
Emerald Street Boys 35
Emerald Street Girls 39
Silver Chain Gang 41

1982
Original Rappin' Three 48
Southside Three 49
West Coast Funk Brigade 51
Baron Von Scratch 53

Sir Lover the MC 56
All City Battle of the Rappers 58
"Ultra Groove" 59
Black Community Festival 61
The Rocket 63

1983
"Christmas Rap" 67
Fresh Tracks Promos 72
KNHC 75
Sounds of Seattle 79
"7 Rainier" 82
"Supersonic Rap" 85

1984
Kings of Cuts 88
"I Pity the Man" 91
Danny Dee Rock 93
Summer Break 97
"Come and Get Some Boys" 98
Rotary Boys' Club Meeting 100
"Rhyme One Time" 102
Cosmic Legion Crew 106
Record Stores 111

1985
Freeze MCs 114
J.O.C. 117
ELP and Impact Productions 118
Love Sick Rhymers 120
JROD 124
Kylea 125
"Documentary Break Dance" 126
"Pig Latin" and "Feel My Beat" 128
Emerald Street Boys Break Up 131
"Square Dance Rap" 133

Bibliography 137
About the Author 141

FOREWORD

By DJ Nasty-Nes

Back when Rap music was born, I already knew it was gonna be big. After studying broadcasting at Bellevue Community College, I started my own radio show in 1981 on 1250 KFOX. I always supported Rap in Seattle, and I was even a DJ for local Hip Hop group Emerald Street Boys. We recorded several intros for my KFOX weekend show called *Fresh Tracks*, the first all-Rap radio show in Seattle.

One memorable Emerald Street Boys performance happened at the 1982 Black Community Festival. It was a really hot day, and there was no tent over the turntables, so the sun was beating down on the black vinyl records. As they got hotter and hotter, they bent and warped so they wouldn't play. Somehow, we finished the show that day, but I learned my lesson about the sun.

I met Sir Mix-A-Lot at a Boys and Girls Club when my good friend Sheila Locke and I went to see him DJ. After that, I played a Mix-A-Lot song called "Let's G" on my show, and my boss Steve Mitchell heard it. He actually pulled me into his office and scolded me for playing it. But I never quit, and I stayed true to the game. I even helped Vitamix get a single deal with Profile Records in 1986.

Everybody in Seattle remembers when "Square Dance Rap" blew up. The success of that song was truly amazing! I'm so proud to have worked at Nastymix Records from the beginning. In 1988, I left KFOX, and I teamed up with my homie "Shockmaster" Glen Boyd to host a new show called *Rap Attack* at 90.3 KCMU (now KEXP). You can hear me on Eazy E's hit song

"Radio," and I was a very early supporter of NWA. I have been doing Hip Hop radio for more than forty years, whether it was over the airwaves or across the internet.

In 1996, I met Novocaine132, who came on my *Rap Attack* show to talk about *The Rocket* music newspaper. When he asked me to write this foreword, I wasn't sure at first. Then I read the book. For *The Birth of Seattle Rap*, Novocaine132 interviewed many of the actual figures of the early Rap days in Seattle.

This book means a lot to me because I know most of the names and faces inside. Many of the artists gave me tapes to play on *Fresh Tracks*. I heard Jam Delight rapping in the early days. I witnessed West Coast Funk Brigade, Frostmaster Chill, Sir Lover the MC, Baron Von Scratch and others performing all through the early '80s. I was even a part of the legendary Cosmic Legion Crew, along with many talented rappers and DJs.

The Birth of Seattle Rap is a really solid history book, so check it out. I'm glad that my friend Novocaine132 put this story together so people can learn about the 206. As I always used to say on my radio show, "Peace, love and Hip Hop unity—stop the gang banging, and stop the violence!"

—DJ Nasty-Nes

ACKNOWLEDGEMENTS

I have been lucky to interview many of the subjects of this book, and there are so many people to thank, including Peter Barnes, Carlos Barrientes, Ronnie Beasley, Marla Beaver, Jeremy Beckwith, Reco Bembry, Tony Benton, Chris Blanchard, David Blanchard, Peter Blecha, Glen Boyd, Keith Brofsky, Danny Clavesilla, Dr. James Croone, Lynn Croone, Ryan Croone, Charles R. Cross (rest in peace), Felicia Cross, Vinny Dom, Wendi Dunlap, Kevin Gardner, Jerome Gibson, Eric Gordon, Douglas Green, Frank Harlan, Bryan Hatfield, Frank Higginbotham, Kerry Hodge, Rcurtis Jamerson, Kevin Jones, Rodney Jones, Ronnie Jones, Mike Joyce, Pete Kuhns, Kristine Larsen, Sheila Locke, Zhonyak Love, Allen Lynch, Dan Magden, Terrence Matthews, Lawrence Moore, Karen Moskowitz, Robert Newman, Bruce Pavitt, David Perry, Anthony Ray, Nestor Rodriguez, George Rush, Marline Russell, Keith Samuels, LaSalle Samuels, Dave Schnuckel, Helene Silverman, Christopher Smith, Steve Sneed, Stephen Spence, Greg Steen, Anthony Steward, Bobby Stills (rest in peace), Mark Sullo, Neil Sussman, Charles Thompson, Michael Turner, Ray Valrey, Thomas Washington, Carol Wells, Steven Wesley, Kevin Westenberg, Erika White, Shamseddin Williams, Lance Wilson and everyone else who contributed. I am very grateful for all your help, and I never would have been able to finish this book without each and every one of you.

I would like to thank the staff at the University of Washington Suzzallo Library's periodicals department for their help in my research of local music history.

Dr. Daudi Abe published an excellent book in 2020 titled *Emerald Street: A History of Hip Hop in Seattle* about the four elements of hip hop and how they are related to Seattle's cultural and social history. *Emerald Street: A History of Hip Hop in Seattle* has been extremely inspiring to me, and it contains an extraordinary amount of information about the Seattle hip hop canon.

Mike Clark, John Funches and Gary Campbell have been exceptionally helpful in doing research for this project, and they deserve special recognition.

To the late Jonathan "Wordsayer" Moore, the "mayor of Seattle hip hop," thank you for the seeds of knowledge you planted in all of us.

And last, a loving thank-you to my wife, Megan, for always believing in me and supporting my dreams.

INTRODUCTION

Welcome to *The Birth of Seattle Rap*. This book is an attempt to document rap music in Seattle from its origins until the end of 1985. It is the result of many conversations with key figures in the scene, and the people who were part of this movement share their memories and experiences. Before we can talk about Seattle, here's a simplified reminder of how hip hop emerged from New York.

Hip hop is traditionally understood to be composed of four distinct art forms: DJing, graffiti, breakdancing and rapping. In New York in the early '80s, these four elements were often presented together; an example can be seen in the film *Wild Style*.

One could argue that the DJ is the foundation of the hip hop culture because of pioneers like Kool Herc. DJs had the sound systems, record collections and cutting skills to rock any party.

Others might say that graffiti was the key to expanding the hip hop message. By writing on trains, spray can artists magically spread the visual aspect of the culture all across the country. These rolling canvases were free overnight delivery systems for images that displayed the work of expert aerosol artists.

Some observe that breakdancing was the fuel for hip hop. Instead of using violence against other gangs to settle turf wars, hip hop artists used breaking as a different way to compete. Trailblazer crews were known to have impeccable tastes in fashion, and they would carry boomboxes in public, blasting hip hop music that sounded fresh and new.

The rap element was also there from the start, and rap certainly was a huge motivator of the scene. As the '80s unfolded, rappers quickly became the high-profile representatives of hip hop. Rappers were easy celebrities to identify, and they amassed fans more quickly than breakdancers, graffiti writers and DJs. Early rappers created imaging and individual style to enhance their appeal.

In Seattle it was no different. We also had DJs, graffiti writers, breakdancers and rappers. *The Birth of Seattle Rap* mostly looks at the rap element of hip hop, but that's not to minimize the contributions of the other three elements—far from it. All the hardworking DJs, graffiti writers and breakdancers in Seattle deserve to be recognized for their amazing work.

As a journalist, my love comes from combing through the lyrics of early rap music. I enjoy seeing how the stories and rhymes reflect the experiences of an entire generation. Hopefully, *The Birth of Seattle Rap* can give a little context to the history of how this rhyming culture began and highlight several people who haven't made it to the history books yet.

A note about Tacoma. Tacoma has such a deep history of hip hop that I feel it deserves its own separate study. I don't want to mix up the Seattle and Tacoma scenes because they are distinct and unique to each other. So, *The Birth of Seattle Rap* will focus on Seattle; it doesn't include Tacoma or other nearby cities.

My love of Seattle-based rap dates to 1988, when tapes of Sir Mix-A-Lot's *SWASS* circulated among my classmates at Blanchet High School. Later, in 1995, I was blessed to write at *The Flavor*, a hip hop magazine. Then after putting in several years work at Tribal Music, promoting a rap compilation called *Do the Math*, I took a break in 2001 to travel and experience life. Now that hip hop culture is more than fifty years old, I want to help tell the story of how rap music in Seattle was born.

The Birth of Seattle Rap is not a complete encyclopedia of everyone who rapped in our city. It is my wish that anyone not mentioned in the book will also have their story told in one way or another. This book is just a small step toward learning the full history of how the revolutionary sound of rap music emerged in Seattle.

—Novocaine132

1980

DISCO BREAKS

In the 1970s, young people across America were drawn to a new type of music called disco. Nightclubs and roller skating rinks hired DJs, who often blended one song into another to the delight of dancers or roller skaters. Seattle was no different, and this exciting musical culture spread quickly. Disco DJs collected rhythmic dance records, anything with a solid beat that could be dropped into the continuous mix.

The Facts was the weekly newspaper for Seattle's Black community, and it printed a music column called "Soul Street." Sylvester Ford was the writer, and he would go around Seattle every week to check out the discos. In an early 1979 column, he wrote, "Disco here, disco there, the fever is everywhere, folks." After mentioning popular hangouts including the Airport Hilton and The Trojan Horse, Ford wrote, "Hey, we are talking about the thing that is taking over in the night spots in our town, disco." When it came to nightclubs, Ford had a few favorites; Bahamas in Pioneer Square, Emmet's in Bellevue and Slim's in Columbia City all received flattering coverage. Slim's DJ at the time was named "Mad Man Bob."

By the fall of that year, Ford had fully embraced this disco culture. "Well folks, nightclub owners try to bring people something different, but most of the time it doesn't work. Disco is here, let's face it," declared Ford with finality in his column.

But then, the very next week, Ford printed what amounted to a retraction. After partying to live music at Slim's, he concluded, "Maybe live music is not dead, thanks to club owners like Slim taking a chance on live music. Disco is good entertainment, don't take us wrong. But we think live music is better." Possibly, he just got a ton of angry responses to his championing of disco.

Disco's domination was also being chronicled in a second publication. *The Rocket*, a monthly newsprint magazine, was the most important music journal in Seattle and had a wide-reaching audience. "Dana Andrews, head of the Electric Canary, a disco and rock record service for clubs, feels that club owners shy away from rock," wrote the paper in 1980.

Record pools like Electric Canary were basically intermediaries between record labels and club DJs. The DJs would get free records from the labels, and the labels would get their songs played in all the hottest clubs, so both sides saw it as a win. Andrews explained his general feeling about Seattle partygoers: "When people want to dance, they want to dance to disco music. There's just not a lot of clubs playing new wave and rock."

Clever DJs utilized R&B and disco records because of their long instrumental breakdowns in the middle of the tracks. Sometimes, these would go on for several minutes. Party promoters or DJs would use these breakdowns to grab the microphone and make announcements or hype up the party. Talented hosts and emcees even put together some off-the-cuff rhyming phrases to say during the breaks.

By using two copies of a record, a DJ could isolate the funky break in the middle of the song and then loop it over and over to make an instrumental track. Perhaps the most famous example of this is "Rapper's Delight" by The Sugarhill Gang. As everyone knows, the music behind "Rapper's Delight" is basically the instrumental breakdown from the middle of "Good Times," by Chic, replayed over and over by other musicians.

DJ Mike Joyce was one DJ who witnessed the transformation from disco to rap. Joyce had always been obsessed with DJ culture and the dance music scene. He remembers going to The Monastery club to hear DJ Dana Andrews (from Electric Canary) mix records. Joyce wouldn't even dance—he would just sit in the booth, listen to the beats and soak up every detail of how to DJ. Around the turn of the decade, Joyce had a gig spinning disco and dance music at The Penthouse, a bar in the Renton Sheraton Hotel. Then he played at Yukon Mining Company in Lakewood until a shooting closed the club down.

In the spring of 1980, a barbecue restaurant called Lateef's opened on Rainier Avenue South. It was managed by a couple named Lester and Pat

Page 6, THE FACTS Week of April 23 through April 29, 1980

Soul Street

by Sylvester Ford

LATEEF's....THERE IS NO PLACE LIKE IT. We are talking about the newest night spot in town, Lateef's, the Barbecue place. Yes, folks, Mr. LESTER GREEN has got one of the most beautiful clubs in the city. You just must get by and see this one of a kind night spot. Lateef's Disco Room is out-of-sight with all the lights flashing. The room is large so people can move around the club. There is also a spacious dance floor. We really got off on that. Friday and Saturday, Lateef's is open until 4:30 AM with Disco and Breakfast and on Thursday, ladies, you can get in free. That's right, free. So this weekend, make Lateef's one of your stopoff places. They have some of the best Barbecue in town and their new Disco place, well. there's just no place else like it.......Still out in the street, we got a chance to stop by KANE's, the place that says it all when it comes to Disco fun. The club was really jumping this past Thurs-

The "Soul Street" column in *The Facts* newspaper. *Image courtesy of Marla Beaver,* The Facts *publisher, from the Seattle Public Library archives, scan by author.*

Green. This was a popular club for the Black community in Seattle, and Lateef's advertised heavily in *The Facts* throughout 1980. Since Joyce needed a new gig, he went and tried out for Lester Green. Joyce showed off his expert cutting and mixing skills, nailing the performance. Green liked what he heard, so he gave Joyce the job, and Joyce DJed at Lateef's for a couple of years.

Joyce remembers very well when "Rapper's Delight" came out. Like many other DJs at the time, he would segue from "Good Times" to "Rapper's Delight," and the dance club patrons loved it. That mix even worked at his gigs in more rural areas and those bars that skewed toward older listeners. "There wasn't any polarization," Joyce recalls about the early '80s scene in Seattle. "There wasn't a feeling of Black music or white music; there was just dance music." The disco scene attracted fans from diverse racial and social backgrounds. Music was a uniting force, and it brought people together.

There were open-mic, pop-up rap battles at Lateef's throughout 1980 and 1981. Some of these were more spontaneous, while others were well organized and promoted. A place where you could do an open mic contest was very appealing to young rappers, and word of Lateef's spread across the city. Some have observed that one reason for this was that Lester Green was never granted a liquor license for the restaurant. This meant that it never became an adults-only establishment, and young people were always allowed to enter.

DJ Mike Joyce recalls participating in a very early rap battle at the Steak Express restaurant, which was another popular place to hear DJs. The promoter was a man by the name of Robin Summerrise. There were four people involved in this particular showdown: Joyce, Eddie "Sugar Bear" Wells, the "Black Englishman" and DJ "Black Nasty." Joyce wrote down some lyrics to perform at the battle to the beat of "Sugar Hill Showdown," and he recalls that the rap contained insults aimed at Black Nasty, who was the DJ at Number One Son's club.

"Kickin" Kevin Jones graduated from Franklin High School in 1979. He remembers that during his senior year, he went to a KYAC Radio remote broadcast at a downtown record store. KYAC was the hottest R&B station in Seattle at that time. The record store was called Wide World of Music, located at Third Avenue and Pike Street, and it was soon bought by the Musicland chain. Jones originally went hoping to win a TV giveaway, and he developed a sneaky plan that involved submitting multiple entry forms. To his surprise, the scheme worked, and Jones won the television.

The host of the live event was KYAC owner Robert Scott, and Scott invited Jones to say a few words on the air. Jones was smooth on the mic announcing the next song, telling the audience, "I just won a new TV!" Then, according to Jones, he continued like a real radio announcer, "The next song is by Ohio Players, and it's called 'Jive Turkey.'" Scott was very impressed. He laughed and said, "Let's hire this kid." Just like that, Jones had found his new passion.

Jones also pursued DJing for parties due to his love of music. He started with two cassette tape decks that he would play though a stereo system, switching from one deck to the other. Then he got community service hours after getting into trouble, which led to his first DJ gig. He was hired to DJ a party at Neighborhood House, a Seattle housing and community services agency. The terms were that Neighborhood House would provide the turntables, but Jones would have to bring his own records. The budget was only fifty dollars to buy records, so he wisely purchased as many full-length LPs as he could afford. He could have bought a greater quantity of seven-inch singles for the money, but the albums had so many more songs. He then used that handful of albums to play music all night, rotating between different artists. It was a success, and his strategy paid off.

"Kickin" Kevin Jones *(left)* and DJ Mike Joyce *(right)*. *Photograph courtesy of Mike Joyce.*

When he heard "Rapper's Delight," he responded to the new rap sound. He also liked Cameo, Jonzun Crew and Jimmy Spicer. Jones knew that Lateef's was a real Seattle hotspot, and he hoped to DJ there. He met Lester Green, who asked him, "Can you mix?" "Sure," said Jones, thinking that mixing meant simply blending songs consecutively. Just like DJ Mike Joyce had done not too long ago, Jones performed for Green. When Jones was done, he thought that the tryout had gone well. Unfortunately, Green did not feel the same way.

Jones asked Green if he had liked the performance, but Green was obviously not impressed. Green frowned and said, "Yeah, it was alright, but can you *mix* though?" Jones didn't know what he meant, so Green said, "Come back this weekend and watch the DJ. He can *mix*." Green let Jones come and sell drinks at Lateef's that Friday. The DJ walked in and started setting up, and suddenly, Jones realized that it was DJ Mike Joyce. He had been to one of Joyce's gigs before and liked his musical taste. After that meeting, Joyce and Jones became good friends and would often appear at club gigs together as a team. Jones got the DJ name of "Kickin" Kevin around this time.

His experience at the TV giveaway left a strong impression on Kickin Kevin. He remained very interested in the radio industry, and in the fall of 1979, he went to Bellevue Community College to study the subject. A local station called KKNW 1510 was experimenting with different formats. Mike Joyce was DJing there, as was another DJ named Ricardo Frazer. Kickin Kevin liked the philosophy of the station, so he joined the team. According to Kickin Kevin, KKNW started accepting mixtapes from local DJs around 1980, and they would play these mixes on the air. Kickin Kevin recalls receiving and broadcasting a number of tapes from one DJ in particular. His name was Nestor Rodriguez.

DJ NASTY-NES AND SHEILA LOCKE

Nestor "DJ Nasty-Nes" Rodriguez was born in Okinawa, Japan, in an army hospital. He grew up in the Philippines and then moved to Seattle and attended Seattle Prep and then Roosevelt High School. Rodriguez went to his first concert, The Osmond Brothers and David Cassidy at the Seattle Center Coliseum, at the age of thirteen. Because of Rodriguez's Filipino identity, his Yesler Terrace neighbors called him the "Crazy Pinoy." He remembers his favorite role models were Muhammad Ali and Bruce Lee. In 1979, Rodriguez finished his last year at Roosevelt High School, but tragedy struck the following year when he lost his mother to cancer.

Around this time, according to Rodriguez, he met a hairstylist at Pacific Nautilus Health Club in Bellevue. She was attending salon school and doing inexpensive haircuts at her house to get more practice, so Rodriguez began occasionally going there for a cheap cut. At the house, the hairstylist's sibling Sheila (formerly known as Ed before her transition in 1995) would sometimes be DJing in another room. Rodriguez could hear the music in the background, and he loved it. So, one day, he asked the hairstylist about the music. After finishing the haircut, she took Rodriguez to the other part of the house and introduced him to Sheila.

Sheila showed Rodriguez the two turntables that she was mixing on, and they quickly became friends. Rodriguez was always obsessed with music and becoming a DJ, but he wanted a new nickname other than "Crazy Pinoy." So instead, he started calling himself "DJ Nestor Rodriguez." Unfortunately, this sounded awfully close to "DJ Mister Rodriguez," so he kept trying new names. He finally decided to incorporate his martial arts nickname "Nasty-Nes" to become "DJ Nasty-Nes."

Sheila Locke attended Bellevue Community College and studied the same radio program that "Kickin" Kevin Jones would take the following year. This led to a job for Locke as an on-air disc jockey at KYAC Radio, hosting the overnight shift in 1979. In another coincidence, as one of the station personalities, Locke had been at the Wide World of Music broadcast where Kickin Kevin had won his free TV.

One night, Locke brought Nasty-Nes to the station to tour the office and see how the job was done, even letting him into the booth while she was broadcasting her show. Nes was excited to see how radio worked, and shortly after that visit to the station, he also enrolled in the broadcasting program at Bellevue Community College.

DJ Nasty-Nes would occasionally travel to New York to visit his sister, whose friend worked for 92 FM WKTU radio. In this manner, Nes was exposed to a ton of early rap songs. According to Nes, he visited the WKTU station office and really admired the DJs, wishing he could be just like them. He purchased as many early rap records as he could find in New York and brought them back to play for his Seattle listening audience.

In the summer of 1981, KYAC went off the air, and the 1250 AM spot on the dial was replaced by KKFX, commonly known as KFOX. DJ Nasty-Nes immediately got a job at KFOX and began his on-air career in Seattle radio. At first, he was only allowed to do the weather, but soon, his responsibilities at the station grew to include his own show.

According to Nes, he played acceptable KFOX format groups such as The Whispers and Lakeside on his weekday show called *Night Beat*, but he would also occasionally play rap. "King Tim the III" and "The Breaks" were two songs he remembers spinning during his first year. He felt that hip hop was so much more than just a fad. People all around Seattle would record his show at home on portable cassette decks and then save the tapes. It was the easiest way to hear the new rap sounds in Seattle at the time.

Steve Mitchell was an early manager at KFOX. Even though he didn't believe that rap should be part of the station brand, Mitchell and Nes eventually made several compromises. Mitchell allowed Nes to host an entire

Sheila Locke (*left*) and Nestor "DJ Nasty-Nes" Rodriguez (*right*). *Movie still from* The Otherside *(2013), courtesy of Vinny Dom and MAD Northwest.*

show every Sunday night dedicated to this new hip hop music. It would be called *Fresh Tracks*. They also agreed that Nes could play two rap songs per hour during the week on *Night Beat* but no more.

Mitchell reflected on that period later in a September 1997 radio show with Nes on KCMU 90.3 FM. That show was the last *Rap Attack* hosted by Nes, since he was moving to California. "For instance, 'Freak a Zoid' by Midnight Starr. Why did I object so much to that record?" Mitchell wondered. "I wouldn't put it on [during] the daytime, but I hear it now and I should have done it. It's a great song," admitted Mitchell. The *Fresh Tracks* show was especially popular with the city's pop-locking, bopping and breakdancing communities.

TERRIBLE TWO

Bopping was basically a predecessor to breakdancing that involved creatively using one's body to express talent and skill. One-on-one or group battles involved dancing against each other, but there was also an element of verbal ranking or insulting that came along with it. These early disses and put-downs evolved to become full rhymes and raps that dancers could use to taunt their opponents.

Nobody ever thought to record these ranking sessions, but they certainly fueled the culture of pure rhyme battles that followed. Eventually, the rhyme element decoupled from the dance element, and rappers would battle with words alone.

The new rapping culture was embraced by kids who were very young; many were still in middle school. "Cap" rapping became a trend at every school and park gathering. You basically wanted to rhyme and insult your opponent to make the crowd laugh.

When "Rapper's Delight" hit, every kid in Seattle was obsessed with it, and suddenly, everyone wanted to be a rapper. Memorizing the lyrics to the song and then saying them back was like a challenge. If you could recite "Rapper's Delight," you had instant status. Some kids even brought the record with them to school.

Dr. James "Captain Crunch" Croone was a major early force in the Seattle bopping scene. Like many kids of his generation, Croone was bussed to a different part of the city from the area in which he lived. This bussing program was designed to increase diversity in the public school system. At

Ingraham High School, he took trumpet lessons, but according to Croone, he never practiced very much. Instead, he became interested in street dancing and learned how to move his body in every direction.

Eddie "Sugar Bear" Wells was a young middle school track star who also enjoyed football. Wells was an only child and took saxophone lessons in school. His mother, Carol, had called him "Bear" since he was young. Carol Wells recalls being in the car driving to California when her family first heard "Rapper's Delight." According to Wells, both she and Bear were immediate fans of this new kind of music.

James Croone was well known as a dancer, and he often crossed paths with a competitor named Johnny Pellum. Neither Croone nor Pellum had nicknames at this point; everyone just called them by their last names. Croone faced off against Pellum one day at Seattle Center. However, Croone had a one-piece jumpsuit on, all white with a Playboy bunny logo on the back. As Croone recalls, it was extremely tight and restricted his movements, causing him to lose that battle. However, Croone got his revenge at a local YMCA the next time they faced off. At the rematch, Croone was comfortably dressed and beat Pellum, regaining his bragging rights as the best dancer in Seattle.

Besides Johnny Pellum, Croone also remembers seeing James "Po Jo" Solomon and Neil "Snake" Gleason in these circles. Snake had a friend named "Mad Dog." Another hip hop character in the bopping circles was Michael "Space Cowboy" McDonald. According to Anthony "Snap" Steward from the group Snap Crackle Pop, "Croone was the best bopper in the town."

Croone tells a story of how his skill at bopping led to a humorous introduction to Bear. The name Croone was becoming well known around the city, but not everyone knew what he looked like. Bear had heard through the grapevine that Croone had some fierce bopping moves. One day, he encountered Croone, but the two didn't exchange names. Because they had never met before, Bear didn't know who he was talking to. During their conversation, Bear asked him if he had heard of a bopper named Croone.

Croone didn't expose his identity to Bear; instead, he decided to have a little fun. Croone slyly asked Bear what he knew about Croone's dance tricks. Bear described the moves that he heard Croone had done in some famous bopping battles. Then Croone smiled and began to show Bear the actual moves in person. Bear was surprised and embarrassed and instantly realized that he was talking to the real James Croone. The two then became friends.

Bear and Croone started hanging out together, and soon, they were a duo of sorts. Their love of music united them. Croone's favorite songs to bop to were "More Bounce to the Ounce," by Roger and Zapp, and "Scorpio," by Dennis Coffey. Bear loved to dance to "The Pop Along Kid," by Shalamar.

Bear was a student at Roosevelt High when he met classmate Marline Russell. According to Russell, she already had a boyfriend, but Bear kept showing interest in her during the '81–'82 school year. Finally, she became single and started dating Bear. Russell remembers being "front and center for all of the events," and she "would accompany Bear on most of his DJ jobs." Bear and Russell spent time with each other's families, and they were very close.

Both Bear and Croone liked bopping, but they also liked to rap. Eventually, they named themselves the Terrible Two. Now that the group had a name, they rebranded their own individual names to match some popular breakfast cereal brands. Bear became Sugar Bear, and Croone chose the name Captain Crunch.

One routine that they practiced involved rapping to the Treacherous Three's "Feel the Heartbeat" instrumental. Captain Crunch remembers that he and Sugar Bear had jackets emblazoned with the name "Terrible Two" on the back.

1981

JAM DELIGHT

Christopher "Boss" Cross was born in 1965 and grew up in West Seattle. Boss Cross was known all around the city as a rap pioneer. According to a 1986 interview, he admitted that he never had any formal musical training.

As Boss Cross put it, "I never had a music lesson; I just figured it all out." His natural ability as an MC was evident. "I was put into a studio and told to go for it. I worked with it, and everyone seemed to like it," he said.

Gary "Jam" Gilmer was born in St. Louis, Missouri, in 1964. According to many sources, Gary Jam was always dressed in the best b-boy styles, such as Lee jeans, Adidas shoes, gold necklaces and a clean white T-shirt.

Journalist Glen Boyd interviewed Gary Jam in 1987 for *The Rocket* newspaper. "Born Gary Gilmer, the St. Louis native has already worked with some of the biggest names in rap," wrote Boyd. Jam explained, "I want to be a good role model for other entertainers, other singers, for the public as well." According to Boyd, "While [Jam] worked on demos with Davy D for labels like Tommy Boy, he rapped in Seattle."

Eventually, the two united and named themselves Jam Delight. Big Boss often wore a white vest with the name "Jam Delight" spelled out down the front. According to a contemporary, Jam Delight had a rhyme that went like this: "Pow! Boogie! We rock all night! Gary Jam and Boss Cross, we're Jam Delight."

One of the early DJs for Jam Delight was a young Anthony "Sir Mix-A-Lot" Ray. In a 2021 interview, Mix-A-Lot remembered, "I used to work with a rap group; they were called Jam Delight. I would produce and make beats and scratch, and [Jam Delight] would put out songs around town."

Christopher "Big Boss" Cross. *Photograph courtesy of* The Rocket, *appeared in* The Rocket *in November 1986.*

Both Terrible Two and Jam Delight were honing their craft. As the groups got better, they eventually had to clash. According to Captain Crunch, the infamous battle happened at Lateef's. When it came time to perform, Terrible Two did their rehearsed rap over the Treacherous Three's "Feel the Heartbeat" instrumental. Jam Delight rapped over the peppier Sugarhill Gang's "Showdown" beat.

Jam Delight were the crowd favorite, and the Terrible Two lost the battle. "[Jam Delight] came out and did their stuff; they were off the hook," remembered Captain Crunch in a 2020 interview. "Ours was too mellow, and we lost it." Terrible Two felt like their instrumental was too slow to rock the Lateef's crowd.

It's very possible that this battle was documented at the time by a writer named Ray Gastil, who wrote for the *Seattle Sun* newspaper. Gastil went to Lateef's late in the summer of 1981 and covered a rap battle for the paper in an article about Seattle rap. "On a Saturday night at Lateef's, home of good barbecue and a disco far south on Rainier Avenue, black teenagers are chanting jive lyrics to a recorded bass line," the piece began.

Gastil went on to describe what he saw at Lateef's that evening: "It's a rap-off contest between five different rap-singing duos. The best is called Jam Delight. Two guys, one tall, one short, work together like a comedy team. They ask for crowd participation and get it. Everyone claps their hands and sings 'ho-oh' back at them." Jam Delight managed to beat four other crews at Lateef's, establishing their dominance in Seattle. The piece ended with a promise of more to come: "Meanwhile, Lester Green and Damien the DJ at Lateef's are planning another rap-off in a few weeks."

Shortly after their loss to Jam Delight, Terrible Two had to take stock. They wanted to become the best in the city. Sugar Bear considered recruiting additional members for their crew. He ran track with another student named

Gary "Jam" Gilmer. *Photograph courtesy of Kevin Westenberg, appeared in* The Rocket *in December 1987.*

Jeremy Beckwith, and the two boys had been friends since childhood. Sugar Bear called Beckwith one afternoon following track practice. They were both fans of New York rappers like Sugarhill Gang and Kurtis Blow, so the conversation turned to hip hop music. "Do you want to rap?" asked Sugar Bear suddenly.

Beckwith hadn't thought about it being a possibility before; it was something that seemed out of reach. His interest in hip hop made it pretty easy to say yes, according to Beckwith. They never brought this idea to Captain Crunch, who doesn't remember seeing Beckwith and Sugar Bear rap together.

Sugar Bear gave Beckwith the name "Sweet J" and even wrote some rudimentary rhymes for Beckwith to rap. "What can I do? What can I say? I go by the name of the incredible Sweet J," went one early example. Beckwith was thrilled to actually perform rap music for the first time.

COSMIC CREW

John "Frostmaster Chill" Funches became interested in music at an early age. While he was growing up, he enjoyed playing hoops with his brother Anthony and watching a TV program called *Zoom*. In fact, *Zoom* featured fun educational segments with rhyming words and verses, which Funches says helped plant the seed of writing poetry and rhymes at an early age. Like Captain Crunch, Funches also took trumpet lessons as a student.

Michael "Mellow Mike" Thomas was part of a large family and had six brothers. Growing up, he had to learn how to be loud to get his fair share of anything. According to a 1982 write-up in *The Rocket*, Thomas's mother told him, "Shut up, boy—you talk too much. Maybe someday it'll bring you some money." He developed a "slow distinctive style," as the piece described it. Thomas also played Rotary Boys' Club basketball.

In 1979, Funches and Thomas were friends. They each chose nicknames; Funches chose "Sir Slam" because he liked basketball, and Thomas chose "Mellow Mike." One day, they encountered notorious rap capper Michael

"Sir Skyy" Simmons. He was one of the legends of the very early rapping scene and also DJed under the name DJ Skyy. His battle technique was to use props in his competitions.

For instance, Sir Skyy would end with a dis or cap about having the battle "locked down" and then pull out a padlock from his pocket and hold it up as everyone laughed and cheered. Sir Skyy was adept at this technique. He might rhyme about his opponent smelling bad and then produce a bar of soap. These cap raps were all about creatively putting down your opponent in front of a crowd.

Michael "Mellow Mike" Thomas. *Photograph courtesy of David Blanchard.*

Sir Skyy was clever when it came to insults, and sure enough, he rap capped both Funches and Mellow Mike. As Funches recalls, they didn't have any good comebacks, so they had to concede.

Funches and Mellow Mike had been beaten, but their humiliation didn't stop them from making an important discovery. At some point after the incident, the two were shopping at Dirt Cheap Records on Twenty-Third Avenue and Union Street. They saw the candy-striped Sugarhill label and bought the record of "Rapper's Delight." When they got home and played it over and over, they both fell in love with this new art form. It was euphoric.

According to Funches, Mellow Mike had the idea first: "I want to write a rap," he exclaimed. But Mike wasn't as good at handwriting or spelling, so he asked Funches to dictate his rap and write it down. Mike practiced it over instrumental beats on their Sanyo boombox. Then Funches wrote a rap too. Both were freshmen at Garfield High School, and they brought the boombox to school the next day. When Sir Skyy, who was a sophomore, came into the room, Mellow Mike and Funches were ready.

With the boombox sitting on the floor and pumping out a beat, Mellow Mike and Funches blasted all their best insults and rhymes at Sir Skyy. It was a major win for Funches and Mellow Mike. But as Funches recalls, the next day, Sir Skyy showed up with his own boombox and a sheet of notebook paper with rhymes on it. He retaliated back at Funches and Mellow, throwing his best insults. Other classmates watched as this rivalry developed.

Finally, the three decided to become a group due to their mutual love of this brand-new thing called rapping. Garfield High School had a talent show called *Bubbling Brown Sugar*, and the three wanted to enter. They called their group Cosmic Crew and practiced for the show after school. But one of their lyrics dissed a student who was a senior. That student heard them rehearsing and complained to the principal that the Cosmic Crew were bullying him. The principal agreed that it was inappropriate and kicked Cosmic Crew out of the *Bubbling Brown Sugar* talent show.

Local Seattle rap historian Mike Clark remembers being in art class at Garfield that year and hearing Mellow Mike and Funches tapping on the table and rapping to the simple improvised beat. That classroom was the first place where Clark had ever seen live freestyle rapping.

Some friends remember Mellow Mike's style being comedy rap, with a few dirty words thrown in for good measure. Mike had spent time in Oakland, the same place that influenced Too Short. According to one fellow musician, Mellow Mike especially liked the instrumental of "Genius of Love," and he created funny, entertaining rhymes to the beat of that track. A Mellow Mike line that always got laughs was, "Your momma got hit by the 48 bus," which referenced a popular Metro transit route. During his sophomore year, Mellow Mike left high school to go into a program called the Job Corps. This left Sir Skyy and Funches as a duo.

Around this time, Funches switched his name from Sir Slam to "Frostmaster Chill." The two had a good chemistry. Sir Skyy had lots of audio equipment, and he had a strong knowledge of how the gear worked. He taught Frostmaster the ins and outs of the hi-fi mixing setup. Skyy also showed Frostmaster how to scratch records. The two made a few rudimentary tapes but nothing too serious.

The pair, Frostmaster Chill and Sir Skyy, eventually went their separate ways. Frostmaster had to spend six months in juvenile detention, which separated him from music for a while. Skyy moved to Renton, later becoming one of the first DJs to spin at Keith Olsen's Encore nightclub.

"I'M LITTLE RAY RAPPER"

In 1977, a Seattle record entrepreneur named Gerald "Jerry" Dennon founded First American Records in Seattle. Right away, First American began releasing a torrent of albums, representing all genres of music. Meanwhile, David "Little Ray Rapper" Perry was a Seattle musician, producer and studio engineer who was making a name for himself. As described in *The*

Facts newspaper's "Soul Street" column and elsewhere, Seattle was home to a thriving disco scene in 1979 and 1980.

Perry produced and mixed a big disco hit by Salazar called "1-2-3" on City Records in 1979. Dana Andrews, the manager of Electric Canary's record pool, was a consultant on "1-2-3" and added it to the pool's distribution list, which greatly expanded the reach of the group. Jerry Dennon was paying attention to Salazar, and in 1980, First American re-released "1-2-3" with a B-side called "Let's Hang On." It was a good decision, and "Let's Hang On" spent nineteen weeks on the *Billboard* magazine "Disco Top 100," reaching a high of no. 21 in February 1981.

David "Little Ray Rapper" Perry. *Photograph courtesy of David Perry.*

Salazar was on a roll, and Perry spent most of that year working on the Salazar material. When he had free time, he might visit one of Seattle's nightclubs, such as the Boren Street Disco. But disco was quickly on the way out. Although *Saturday Night Fever* had dominated the Grammys in February 1979, the Disco Demolition Night at Comiskey Park occurred only four months later, in June. At that famous Chicago riot, baseball fans expressed their displeasure toward disco music in a violent outburst, some actually burning the records in toxic bonfires.

Salazar recorded at Pacific West Recorders studio, which was located in a private home near Lake Sammamish. Later, it was moved to Redmond and changed names to become Triad Studio. Perry had access to the studio, and he was intrigued by the new rap sounds of The Sugarhill Gang, Kurtis Blow and Blondie coming out of New York. In 1980, he decided to record his own rap-inspired track.

First, he needed a name, and he chose "Little Ray Rapper." He rapped slowly and then sped up the tape on playback, which created what he termed a "munchkin" effect for the vocals. In fact, The Chipmunks, a popular cartoon band that had gone dormant in 1969, used a similar technique. In 1980, the concept was reintroduced with an album called *Chipmunk Punk*, which may have had an influence, subconscious or otherwise, on Little Ray Rapper.

Little Ray Rapper hired two musicians, Moyes Lucas on drums and Steve Allen on bass, and they laid down their first track, with Little Ray Rapper playing guitar and providing the vocals. "Get That Future Punk" told a story of a down-on-his-luck guy going out to meet women and his humorous experiences in that category. Little Ray Rapper rhymed about how music can be a source of stability in tough times.

Excerpt:

I'm a dancing fool, I was born to be cool, I'm a bona fide ladies' man
I've got the gift of gab and I drive a cab, but yesterday I got canned
Now I'm down and out, and I wanna shout, but I'm holding on to my pride
Cause this funky stuff is just enough to keep me hanging in for the ride

Well, it's time for me to go, and I want you to know that I love this music you hear
And if you love it too, what I want you to do before you buy another beer
Is save that dollar until tomorrow, and go to the record store
And buy my album, and make me a star so I no longer will be poor

© *1981 Little Ray Rapper*

Little Ray Rapper liked the result, so he went back into the studio and recorded a second track called "I'm Little Ray Rapper," with singer Dee Daniels providing backing vocals. The two tracks were similar, and "I'm Little Ray Rapper" revealed more about the persona. The character of Little Ray Rapper was very short, hence the name. He also presented himself as an "everyman" type, which implied he was humble and ordinary, allowing the listeners to identify with him.

Excerpt:

I say good things come in little sizes, and with me that's especially true
I may be short, but I've got a great big heart to give to you
I can love you like no other man, I've got that special gift
And I can look right into your eyes with just a little lift

I say just because I'm a little guy, people try to push me around
But if they could see me walking down the street with you, they'd be jealous of what I've found

© *1981 Little Ray Rapper*

It was different than the boastful raps put out by The Sugarhill Gang and other rappers. Little Ray Rapper clearly wanted to make sure that humor was a big part of his brand.

"I'm Little Ray Rapper." © *1981 First American Records, scan by author.*

With two tracks under his belt, he continued recording. Little Ray Rapper completed six more songs in that series of sessions during 1980 and 1981, for a total of eight songs. He submitted "Get That Future Punk" and "I'm Little Ray Rapper" to Jerry Dennon at First American, who liked the tracks. First American agreed to release a single with "I'm Little Ray Rapper" on the A-side, and "Get That Future Punk" on the B-side. The record came out in 1981 on vinyl 7-inch and 12-inch.

Jack Robinson was a successful record producer who lived in Paris and worked with a French label called Barclay. Robinson was born in Seattle, and while he was back for a visit in 1981, he heard "I'm Little Ray Rapper." Robinson subsequently decided that the material was a perfect fit for the Barclay label. A deal was soon drawn up to license the "I'm Little Ray Rapper" single for release in France that same year. Many copies of the Barclay version still exist, while the First American edition is rarer.

Little Ray Rapper was thrilled at the success of his songs, and he made plans to release a full album in 1982 with the title *Get That Future Punk*. But suddenly, according to Little Ray Rapper, First American declared bankruptcy, and Dennon closed the office with no notice. And that was how the story abruptly ended for Little Ray Rapper.

Just because this project never saw a public release at the time, David Perry didn't quit as a musician. In fact, he continued writing and producing music for himself and other artists throughout the '80s. In 1985, Perry gathered dozens of Pacific Northwest and Seattle celebrities to record "Give Just a Little," a fundraiser song similar to "We Are the World."

SIR MIX-A-LOT

Over on Yesler Way, in the Bryant Manor apartments, a young whiz kid was teaching himself about electronics. Anthony "Sir Mix-A-Lot" Ray was a student at Roosevelt High School. He credits Roosevelt with exposing him to new technology and resources. But obtaining these resources required sacrifices, and just like Captain Crunch, he had to wake up before sunrise to stand and wait for the school bus. According to Ray, these long early morning commutes were difficult as a young high school student.

Nestor "DJ Nasty-Nes" Rodriguez also went to Roosevelt, and Ray remembers being intimidated by Nes's tough persona. "The first time I saw Nes, he had a switchblade in one hand and a joint in the other," Ray joked in a 2017 interview. Nes looked tough because he always wore tight muscle shirts and rocked dark sunglasses.

(*Left to right*) Anthony "Sir Mix-A-Lot" Ray, Nestor "DJ Nasty-Nes" Rodriguez and Tracy Kamimae. *Photograph courtesy of Sheila Locke.*

As a young man, Ray liked technology and gadgets. He would take things apart and put them back together. One day at home, just for fun, Ray rewired a set of toy walkie-talkies. He purchased a crystal radio receiver at Radio Shack, which allowed him to listen to signals from other states. This taught him about radio broadcasting and the power of sound. He graduated from high school in 1981, at the young age of seventeen.

Ray began to experiment daily with music in his bedroom, and he recorded broadcasts, especially from the brand-new station called KFOX, which replaced KYAC in 1981. DJ Nasty-Nes would play the newest records from New York, and KFOX was the main place to hear rap in Seattle. In fact, according to Ray, he became so familiar with Nes's voice that he began to imitate it. Some of Ray's earliest raps sounded very similar to the on-air radio voice used by Nes.

Ray's love of electronics led to a job at the Lectric Palace video game arcade at Seattle Center. The manager of Lectric Palace was a man named Greg Jones, and he was the one who hired Ray. Occasionally, Ray would troubleshoot the pinball machines when they broke. "I would go in there and replace capacitors, resistors and power supplies," he says. "As a matter of fact, the job helped me to buy gear."

After leaving Lectric Palace, Ray worked at a company called Transport Equipment. "Even though it paid better, it was the worst job I ever had. That's when I had to wear overalls and dump garbage," says Ray. Despite holding these unglamorous jobs, Ray always kept his dream alive. His dad bought him his first car, a 1969 Buick that cost $300, a couple years after graduation. "I had to put antifreeze in it every day," he recalls.

As he began to develop his identity as a musician, Ray chose his first nickname: "Spaceman." It fit because he liked electronic futuristic-sounding music and saw himself as an explorer.

SNECO

Steve Sneed and Reco Bembry were two artistic-minded men who saw the potential of rap music very early on. As students, they shared an art class at Garfield High School. According to a *Social Sciences Show* interview in 2021, Bembry remembered that Sneed "always had something funny to say." The way Sneed recalls it, Bembry was actually the comical one. "He would tease certain teachers if their afros weren't perfectly combed," laughs Sneed. The two played together in a drumming band called The Ogundas. Sneed and Bembry drummed with passion and had a friendly rivalry that extended to the school baseball team.

Sneed attended the University of Washington, and around 1980, he began taking his educational theater training into the local Black community. Sneed was interested in mentoring young people, including his nephew Eddie "Sugar Bear" Wells, who was finding success as one half of the Terrible Two rap group. Bembry enrolled at Cornish College and studied music. "Music, arts and drama were at the forefront of change in society," recalled Bembry in the 2021 interview.

They eventually came up with a name, "SNECO," that combined the names "Sneed" and "Reco." SNECO began working on music and theater productions that would convey messages of positivity for youth. In the early days, Bembry was the musical director, and Sneed handled the stage side. Through their efforts, the two created gathering spaces for young people to come and practice acting or music for free.

In fact, Anthony "Sir Mix-A-Lot" Ray remembers, "Reco Bembry was the reason I got into music." Ray was playing basketball at the community center, and Bembry showed up to do a musical demonstration for the young people. There were actual keyboards, and Bembry showed everyone how to play a chord or how to make a drumbeat. Ray was entranced, especially when Bembry played the melody from the popular Orbit song "The Beat Goes On." Immediately, Ray knew he wanted to study production, and to do that, he had to get a keyboard. However, a state-of-the-art keyboard could cost a couple thousand dollars, which obviously was out of reach for many families.

The city's young people needed places to express themselves creatively, and SNECO continued their various after-school programs at many locations. The informal classes gave kids instruction in theater, dance and music. This included rapping, so SNECO became one of the early incubators for the blossoming rap culture in Seattle.

SNECO were very busy in 1981. From July 3 to July 19, they put on a play called *Street Life*, which was written by James Lollie. The story centered on young people dealing with the pressures of growing up. Sneed remembers that, thanks to funding from the Boys and Girls Club, the play had a budget of nearly $20,000. Terrible Two and another student named Rcurtis Jamerson were selected to be actors in the play. However, Jamerson didn't want to participate in all the practicing and rehearsals, so he dropped out of the cast. Captain Crunch and Sugar Bear both delivered rap-inspired

(*Clockwise from the top*) Darcell Hubbard, Carol Wells, Reco Bembry and Steve Sneed. *Photograph courtesy of Steve Sneed.*

lines in the performance. Sneed remembers that there was live music to accompany the rap dialogue.

Street Life was advertised in both *The Seattle Times* and *The Seattle Post Intelligencer* on July 3. In *The Times*, the play's title was inaccurate: "*Street Happenings* Musical by James *Lollig* [sic], with music by Reco Bembry," read the listing. *The Post Intelligencer*'s info for the play was more thorough: "*Street Life*, the musical by James Lollie and the Central Area Boys and Girls Club is staged Thurs. through Sat. at 8pm, and Sun at 7pm. Through July 19. A matinee is held Jul. 11 at 2pm. Broadway Performing Arts Building, Seattle Central Community College."

EMERALD STREET BOYS

Rcurtis "Sweet J" Jamerson was born in 1965 and grew up in Seattle. He lived in Los Angeles for two or three years from sixth to eighth grade. Jamerson liked to sing and auditioned for the school band. After returning to Seattle, he joined with some high school friends, and they called themselves The Funkatizers.

One night, Jamerson was listening to the radio when he heard "Rapper's Delight" on KYAC. "I thought it was a commercial, but it just kept going and going," remembers Jamerson. This was a seismic event for the listeners. Every time "Rapper's Delight" came on, kids would turn up the radio and recite the lyrics to the beat. According to Jamerson, he often heard the song down the street, emanating from various neighbors' homes, and he was immediately intrigued by this new music called rap.

Jamerson remembers being at a high school track meet when he first heard Eddie "Sugar Bear" Wells do a rap. The two had both practiced some raps at home, and at the track meet, they decided to test their verses on each other. Jamerson went first, and he remembers his raps were pretty weak. Then Sugar Bear had his turn, and he blew Jamerson's mind with his clever rhymes and wordplay. Sugar Bear clearly won the display at the track meet. "How can I do that?" wondered Jamerson.

Sugar Bear and Jamerson remained friends, and in fact, Sugar Bear wrote short rhymes for both of them. One night, Jamerson went to a social gathering at his uncle's house. There was a microphone, and Jamerson rapped on the mic. He said a few lines of his own and then recited the raps that Sugar Bear had taught him. Someone created a tape of this party, which got passed around the neighborhood. News of the tape made its way to Captain Crunch, who hadn't been there that night. Crunch recognized the lyrics as Sugar Bear's and decided to learn who the rapper was so he could talk to him. He found Jamerson at a house in the Rainier Valley. Jamerson remembers that someone called out, "Hey, Croone [Captain Crunch] is outside!" Jamerson went outside to speak with him, and there was a confrontation.

Captain Crunch quickly figured out that Jamerson was the guy who had dropped out of *Street Life*. Crunch and Sugar Bear concluded that the three could be stronger together than they were separate. Jamerson remembers Sugar Bear called him on the phone shortly after the meeting and said, "We're doing this group. Are you in or out?" Jamerson replied, "Count me in," and became the official third member of the crew. Sugar

(*Left to right*) Eddie "Sugar Bear" Wells, Dr. James "Captain Crunch" Croone and Rcurtis "Sweet J" Jamerson. *Photograph courtesy of Dr. Croone.*

Bear really liked the name "Sweet J" and had already used it for Jeremy Beckwith. But Beckwith had never joined Terrible Two; he was just friends with Sugar Bear.

Since Jamerson had a "J" in his name, Sugar Bear christened him as the new "Sweet J," ignoring the fact that there were now two Sweet Js. The unnamed trio was composed of Sugar Bear, Captain Crunch and Jamerson as "Sweet J."

Because there were three rappers, they could no longer go by Terrible Two. During 1981, the Seattle Convention and Visitors Bureau held a nickname contest for Seattle. Newspapers reported that its old nickname, the "Queen City," was going to be changed. The winner, who turned out to be a Californian named Sarah Sterling-Franklin, was announced in September 1981. Her winning entry was, the "Emerald City."

Captain Crunch remembers the three of them sitting in Sugar Bear's living room trying to come up with name ideas. As the rappers discussed options, they tried out "Emerald City Boys," but it just didn't sound right. Sugar Bear considered the name and repurposed it to create "Emerald Street Boys." This choice showed their pride in their home city of Seattle.

The first mention of Emerald Street Boys in *The Rocket* newspaper appears in the January 1982 issue. An article about Seattle radio station KNHC by

Robert Newman said, "The station has even played a rap by local rappers Emerald Street Boys."

SNECO Productions began with Steve Sneed and Reco Bembry, but soon it grew to four people. Darcell Hubbard became the stage manager, and she would act as a liaison between the venues and the actors or musicians. Meanwhile, Sugar Bear's mother, Carol Wells, managed the legal side of things and made sure that contracts were signed before any performances. Wells was essentially the business manager for Emerald Street Boys.

Sneed would emcee Emerald Street Boys live shows, introducing the group and razzing up the crowd. Bembry usually operated the sound board of the club, making sure that the music sounded just right for the rappers to do their best.

As Emerald Street Boys became more well known, Darcell Hubbard also took on the role of helping choreograph dance routines and creating dramatic stage presences for the three rappers. Emerald Street Boys learned how to move in unison like their heroes, The Temptations.

Reco Bembry remembers there was a live backing band for early Emerald Street Boys shows, and then the group made the switch to rapping over instrumental records. The three members had gone to KFOX to give their music to DJ Nasty-Nes, and they struck up a quick friendship. Soon, Nes became the DJ for their live shows, standing at a table behind them onstage as they performed.

Around this time, a monumental photo shoot occurred for Emerald Street Boys. The photographer was Kristine Larsen, and her location was the Westin Hotel in Downtown Seattle. She captured dozens of stylish images that would essentially become the press kit for the band. An iconic image of the three rappers standing in a round glass skybridge stood out for its symmetrical balance and futuristic composition.

In March 1982, *The Rocket* again mentioned that KNHC was playing an Emerald Street Boys song. According to the paper, the track included the lyric, "Like a Rubik's Cube you gotta figure me out." One of the group's earliest live shows as Emerald Street Boys occurred that same month at the National Guard Armory. The March article listed a date of April 2 for an upcoming show at Sunday's, a bar on Queen Anne Hill. There are also references to recent Emerald Street Boys shows at Fisherman's Restaurant on Pier 57 and the Nighthawk restaurant in South Seattle.

Sugar Bear was always experimenting, trying to learn as much as he could. One of his friends, Bobby "MC 3-D" Stills, remembers Bear's genius revelations. According to MC 3-D, Sugar Bear realized that he could plug a microphone cord into the left channel of a receiver and plug the turntable or tape deck into the right channel. If it was the correct type of receiver with a mono setting, Bear could switch to mono and hear both the microphone and music coming through the same signal. By recording the combined signal out of the receiver, Bear could make demo tape versions of raps right in his own bedroom, with no need for a recording studio.

One day, Emerald Street Boys had set up in a park near Thirty-Fourth Avenue and Cherry Street and were rapping to a boombox. Three or four girls were there to hang out and watch. A young man walked up to them and started bragging that he was a DJ from New York who loved hip hop. He had heard the echoes of Emerald Street Boys' rapping from his aunt's house and had simply followed the amplified sound to the park. His name was Lance "DJ Lee" Wilson from the Bronx. DJ Lee had grown up in New York but spent part of each year in Seattle. In New York, he was a firsthand witness to the birth of rap and the explosion of hip hop culture.

At the park that day, DJ Lee kept telling them that he was hot on the turntables. Emerald Street Boys were a little skeptical but finally agreed to hear him mix. They packed up their gear and went back to Sugar Bear's house. As DJ Lee recalls, everybody was crammed into a small room, and all the chairs were taken so people were also sitting on the bed. He was determined to impress the group, so he asked for "doubles." But they laughed at him because nobody had yet heard that terminology. Lee explained it meant two copies of the same record, but Bear didn't have doubles.

Then DJ Lee remembers asking for "Good Times," which Bear had, and "Bounce Rock Skate," which was also handed to him. With the two matching beats, he knew he could do a routine, but when he tried, the vibrations of the turntable's tonearm caused the needle to skip. Everyone was unimpressed, but then DJ Lee had an idea. "Who has some change?" he asked. They laughed again, but someone had a nickel or a few quarters. DJ Lee put the coins over the needles, and the weight held them down enough for him to do a short routine. He matched the beats together and then cut and juggled them back and forth. Emerald Street Boys were amazed.

Sugar Bear asked DJ Lee if he wanted to DJ for Emerald Street Boys, and Lee informally agreed. He never became a full-fledged member of the group, but he practiced with them a few times and hung out. DJ Lee remembers spinning records at Lateef's, and Emerald Street Boys would occasionally rap there, too. But since DJ Lee lived in Bellevue, a nearby city located across Lake Washington, it was hard to stay truly connected to the group.

A poster for an Emerald Street Boys show, September 17, 1982. *Poster courtesy of 206Zulu, photograph by author.*

According to the new Sweet J, Emerald Street Boys played a house party at Thirty-First and Howell Streets, and the plan for this party was out of the ordinary. Sugar Bear had the idea to bring a lot of television sets into the house and a bunch of power strips to plug them all in. There were TVs everywhere, all over the rooms, which made it feel like an MTV studio or something. The TVs were heavy, and it wasn't easy to set it all up. But when they were done, it was a futuristic party, with TV screens everywhere.

The group hosted a "Back to School Disco" at Campfire House on September 17, 1982. Campfire House was a community agency similar to Neighborhood House, but instead of housing, Campfire House was focused on after-school and summertime activity camps for young people. The poster for the show, which was drawn by Captain Crunch, included a teddy bear logo for DJ Sugar Bear and an eight-sided cut emerald gemstone with the Seattle skyline silhouetted in the middle of it. It cost $2.50 to get in.

EMERALD STREET GIRLS

Mia "Angel Face" Black was the founding member of Emerald Street Girls. The group was associated with Emerald Street Boys, and they would often perform together. Doretha "Playmate" Johnson was the second member of the group. Early in her career, Johnson went by "Lady Di," the common nickname for Diana, Princess of Wales. For a while, Emerald Street Girls were a duo of just the two young ladies.

Bobbie "Luscious Lynn" Solomon always had a musical background, singing in gospel choir and playing the flute while growing up. She attended Nathan Hale High School in the north end of Seattle. When "Rapper's Delight" came out, she loved it just as much as all the boys, and she did her best to memorize the rhymes in the epic song. Rapping was the ultimate hobby, and she started putting verses together, naming herself "Luscious Lynn."

Soon, Luscious Lynn met two friends with similar interests, Jenell "Black Velvet" Cole and another young woman named "Short Cake," who also rapped. They named themselves Luscious Trio. Luscious Lynn and her mom lived near the intersection of Martin Luther King Jr. Way and Cherry Street in the heart of Seattle's Central District, and often, her house would be the hangout spot for the group to practice. Lynn remembers performing as the Luscious Trio on stage at Empire Plaza.

Mia "Angel Face" Black (*left*) and Doretha "Playmate" Johnson (*right*). *Photograph courtesy of Dr. James Croone.*

Eventually, Emerald Street Girls and Luscious Trio met, and they decided to merge into one supergroup. However, Short Cake left around this time and never became part of the new alliance. Emerald Street Girls were now a four-woman crew to be reckoned with. According to Dr. Abe in his book *Emerald Street*, "[Emerald Street Girls] performed intricate choreographed dance routines with their rhymes during live shows at the Black Community Festival and historic Washington Hall." Luscious Lynn remembers doing rap routines at Skoochies nightclub at least once during this time. She also remembers the show at Washington Hall.

One of Luscious Lynn's happy memories is riding with the other Emerald Street Girls in a classic Austin-Healey car through the Black Community Parade. The girls waved at everyone and got some visibility for their group. As Dr. Abe put it, "Although the group soon disbanded and went their separate ways, the significance of Emerald Street Girls cannot be overlooked." "As much as the Emerald Street Boys helped innovate Seattle hip hop, Angel Face, Playmate, Luscious, and Velvet were also pioneers who ensured that an element of gender diversity was present in the early local scene," concluded Dr. Abe.

SILVER CHAIN GANG

LaSalle "Duke of Earl" Samuels moved from Oklahoma to Seattle in 1978, and he attended Nathan Hale High School. As rap was exploding in New York, Samuels paid close attention to all the releases that came out. He would sit in his room with a blank tape in his cassette deck and record rap songs from the radio. Then he could listen to the songs whenever he wanted and could learn the lyrics by rapping them to himself.

Samuels was in a school program called Upward Bound, and he was scheduled to meet periodically with a math tutor. But Samuels would skip those tutoring appointments and go hide behind the school building, listening to rap tapes on his portable deck. Then he would go home and fib to his mom about attending the session.

His first rap names were "Wonder Man" and "Iron Man." Then he heard *Songs in the Key of Life* by Stevie Wonder, with a song called "Sir Duke." He liked the name and took it as his nickname. But when another song stuck in Samuels's mind, the 1962 classic by Gene Chandler called "Duke of Earl," he finally decided his rap name would be "Duke of Earl."

Duke of Earl met a fellow hip hopper named Ernest "Too Cool" Allen. They were both very excited about the culture and formed a loose duo. They practiced after school, trading rhymes back and forth, and decided to name their group "Chain Reaction." As Chain Reaction, the two performed at outdoor parties and schools like TT Minor, Roosevelt and Garfield.

According to Duke, Too Cool was a pretty good rapper but he didn't see it as a career. He was more into the girls and the fast life that rap brought than the actual rhyming to a beat. Duke didn't see it that way. Duke wanted to pursue this as far as he could; as he recalls, "it was like an obsession."

Steven "Sir Wes" Wesley grew up at Nineteenth Avenue and Cherry Street, on the same street where jazz singer Ernestine Anderson resided. His household was religious, and he was a self-described nerd who loved comic books. During his eighth grade school year, his family spent time in Los Angeles, and he attended junior high there.

Wesley was a very dedicated student, and he had saved all his homework and class materials from his previous year in Seattle. It turned out that those materials were now being taught in his new California class, so he breezed through. Not only that, but Wesley was very popular because he could share the answers with his classmates before the tests.

He met a bunch of pop lockers and breakdancers. One of the most influential of these kids was Brian Rosby, who was part of the Star Line

Dancers crew. The trend among the Star Line members was to put a "Sir" in front of their names, so everyone called Brian "Sir Rosby." One day, Sir Rosby told Wesley he needed to get a hip hop name. "We'll call you Sir Wes," said Brian, and the name was born.

When Sir Wes heard "Rapper's Delight," everything changed for him. In 1980, he entered Roosevelt High School and simultaneously fell in love with the rapping culture. Sir Wes had also been friends with rapper Too Cool from Chain Reaction. The two of them sometimes rapped together, and they named their informal duo Too Tight.

Too Tight got their first gig, and they went on stage to perform. According to Sir Wes, when it was time for him to rap, he got some stage fright and didn't do very well. Too Cool was better in front of a crowd. Sir Wes and Too Cool stopped doing music together. Around this time, Too Cool introduced Sir Wes and Duke of Earl, and the two became good friends right away.

Duke of Earl and Sir Wes rapped as a duo for a while, and then they added a third member. Craig "Jazzy D" Daniels grew up near Sir Wes, and they were friends. Daniels loved Star Wars toys and various Saturday morning cartoons. Sir Wes remembers that Daniels once built a realistic-looking lightsaber from parts of a vacuum cleaner. Sir Wes and Daniels both felt like nerds, but when they rapped, they could become someone

(*Left to right*) LaSalle "Duke of Earl" Samuels, Steven "Sir Wes" Wesley, Craig "Jazzy D" Daniels. *Photograph courtesy of Pete Kuhns, appeared in* The Rocket *in December 1982.*

else. Daniels was especially shy in real life, but on the mic, he acted much more like an extrovert.

When he was drafted into the group, Daniels was going by the name "Cool Craig Dee," but there was already a New York rapper called Kool Moe Dee from Treacherous Three, so Daniels needed a new name. Duke of Earl suggested "Jazzy D," and it stuck. Right away, Duke and Wes could tell that Jazzy D was extremely talented. They both remember Jazzy D as the best rapper of the trio. He was always dressed better than anyone. In fact, his jeans were ironed so flat, with a crease in the front and back, that he got the nickname "Plank Man."

Around that time, they named the group "Silver Chain Gang." The name incorporated the word *chain* from Chain Reaction but flipped it in a new way. They still didn't have a DJ, but they had lots of routines to instrumentals that they could perform at parties without a DJ. "It's Magic," "8th Wonder" and "Simon Says" were three examples. They could just put the record on and then do their raps. Duke of Earl wished that Silver Chain Gang could have a DJ on stage with them like Grandmaster Flash or Grand Wizard Theodore—someone who could cut and scratch.

Sir Wes remembers riding the bus with Jazzy D one day. They were "ranking" on each other, and Wes was doing most of the ranking. *Ranking* was just another word for insulting or capping on each other. Jazzy D sat there while Wes pelted him with insults. Then suddenly, Jazzy made his comeback and started capping on Sir Wes with rank after rank. Jazzy D relentlessly mocked the custom-made Michael Jackson glove and the popular "Thriller"-style jacket that Sir Wes was wearing. In fact, Jazzy had the whole bus laughing after he called Sir Wes a Michael Jackson copycat. Wes had to admit that he had lost the insult battle, and he was embarrassed for the rest of the ride.

Duke of Earl became friends with Sugar Bear, and sometimes, he would even get invited to rap sessions with Emerald Street Boys. As Duke recalls, they would sit in a circle around the boombox, and Sugar Bear would insert an instrumental cassette and then press play. Whoever was in the circle that day would take turns rapping without a microphone over the beat.

Sir Wes remembers the moment when he realized Silver Chain Gang had to step up their stage show. He was at a rap-off one day, and Emerald Street Boys showed up to lurk in the crowd. Since Emerald Street Boys weren't part of the announced lineup, everyone relaxed. They were just wearing their regular street clothes and hairnets, looking casual. But then suddenly, after everyone else had performed, the Boys were onstage.

The crowd watched in amazement as Captain Crunch, Sugar Bear and Sweet J started rapping and peeling off their ordinary clothing at the same time, revealing that they were actually wearing matching stage costumes underneath their decoy clothes. Sir Wes was very impressed and determined that Silver Chain Gang was going to learn some of these tricks, too. He approached Captain Crunch and asked him about the trick. "It's showmanship, see?" explained Captain Crunch.

Meanwhile, Silver Chain Gang searched and searched for a DJ. They met a disco DJ named Gustavo, but he wasn't a good fit, so they parted ways after just a couple of shows together. The next DJ they auditioned was Victor "DJ Starchild" Clark. He was primarily a show promoter who was dialed in to all the best spots for parties. Starchild was a mover and a shaker, but unfortunately, he was into the fast life of drugs and drinking. Silver Chain Gang were still young, and they had musical goals. According to Duke of Earl, they didn't want to waste their potential, and luckily, they avoided the perils of the hard partying scene. But that meant that Starchild also wasn't a good fit for their group as a DJ or a manager.

Sugar Bear was friends with Duke of Earl, and one day, Sugar Bear told him about DJ Lee. DJ Lee had never become an official member of Emerald Street Boys, and he was unaffiliated with any crew at the time. Duke of Earl decided to give DJ Lee a try, and Sugar Bear arranged for them to meet. DJ Lee showed up with a backpack, and inside it were a bunch of New York tapes and flyers, authentic and rare rap stuff. As Duke of Earl remembers, he stared at the treasure trove for a long time, carefully memorizing the look and style of each individual item.

DJ Lee recalls that he had literally gotten the tapes from Afrika Bambaataa himself. Bambaataa had hired DJ Lee to do some flyer lettering for him back in the Bronx, and the payment was in rap tapes. DJ Lee loved to draw, and he had practiced various lettering styles that were popular on rap flyers. DJ Lee and Duke of Earl cherished this cassette collection, and they were able to familiarize themselves with all the cutting-edge New York raps of the time.

Duke of Earl and DJ Lee enjoyed shopping for records together all over Seattle. It was all about the hunt for the most exquisite breaks they could rap over. One store they patronized was Golden Oldies in Lake City. Duke of Earl remembers finding doubles of *Did You Heard Me?* by Rufus Thomas, which featured the song "Funky Penguin." They got home and put the two copies on the turntables. DJ Lee was able to isolate the break into a 4/4 rhythm and then repeated it over and over. Duke and the rest of the Silver Chain Gang rapped live over the break, and it was magic. Duke had a feeling that his dreams were literally turning into reality. Soon, they were calling themselves "The Silver Chain Gang Featuring Grandmaster DJ Lee."

A woman rapper named "Foxy" briefly joined the group. She performed several times at live shows, which was unusual in the male-dominated scene at the time. Other women Duke remembers were a solo artist named Special D and a group called The Groovy Gangster Girls. In fact, Duke was so taken by The Groovy Gangster Girls that he formed his own girl group called Nasty Girls. There were three of them, Shannon, Laura and Denise. Duke wrote a rhyme routine to the Jonzun Crew song "Pac Jam," which Nasty Girls rapped in front of a crowd at a Campfire House party.

Saturday, November 13, 1982, was the On the Boards theater group's fifth anniversary party at Washington Hall. On the Boards was celebrating five years of live local theater in Seattle and wanted some modern music for their audience. Emerald Street Boys performed, along with Silver Chain Gang, Emerald Street Girls and a solo rapper named Silky D. *The Rocket* newspaper ran a big piece about the event, with a Kristine Larsen photograph of Emerald Street Boys in the Garfield gymnasium.

The event was held at Washington Hall, a celebrated event space for live performances. The red and yellow poster for the show included another Kristine Larsen photograph, this one showing Emerald Street Boys standing in front of what looks like a classroom chalkboard.

According to Duke of Earl, Jazzy D asked him, "Are we getting paid for this?" Duke of Earl had to explain that although the gig was unpaid, it was excellent publicity for Silver Chain Gang. Duke knew that rappers had to pay their dues to get to the top.

Silver Chain Gang started hanging out at John "Frostmaster Chill" Funches's basement. During one memorable hangout, according to Duke of Earl, Frostmaster cued up two copies of Billy Squier's song "The Big Beat," while Jazzy D and Duke of Earl rapped over that rhythm. Duke became good friends with Frostmaster, and they made demo tapes together. Frostmaster remembers the meticulousness with which Duke would tend to his notebooks. Duke had a million notebooks, and the lines of rhymes were neatly written, almost mechanical in their perfection.

Silver Chain Gang were one of the only groups with the stage show to compete with Jam Delight or Emerald Street Boys. Many local entrepreneurs wanted to manage them, including a businessman named Russell who ran Musicland. DJ Starchild also wanted the job, but the group resisted. According to DJ Lee, they just liked running wild and never signed to a management deal.

A poster for the On the Boards fifth anniversary party, November 13, 1982. The poster includes a photograph by Kristine Larsen, and it was designed by Helene Silverman. *Poster courtesy of Dr. James Croone, photograph by author.*

Duke remembers a number of routines they performed. As far as he knows, few if any of these raps were ever recorded to cassette. Their song "Shasta" was a big hit. It was originally titled "We're Back," and they performed it to the instrumental of "Simon Says," by Sequence. Other Silver Chain Gang songs included "The Verdict," to the beat of "It's Magic," by The Fearless Four; "Do It To It," to the beat of "Do It Do It," by the Fearless 4; "Yes We Can Screw," to the beat of "Yes We Can Can," by the Treacherous Three; "Silver Chain Gang Rocks the Spot"; and "Jazzy D Goes Off."

Duke of Earl's family moved to a new neighborhood, and he began hanging with the Franklin High School crowd. He still maintained his friendships with Sir Wes, Jazzy D and DJ Lee, but the group was shifting. Sir Wes wanted a live band to accompany them, while Duke was resolute that his concept was to keep their DJ. Duke of Earl and Sir Wes could never quite agree, and the tension simmered.

Finally, Silver Chain Gang broke up because of the members' different creative goals. The breakup was slow, and the group faded away. Jazzy D changed his name to "Funky Fresh Jazz," and he began working with Sir Mix-A-Lot. Later, Sir Wes and DJ Lee were hired by Steve Sneed to do a rap to educate Seattle students about energy conservation. The title of the 1987 rap was "Reduce Your Bills and Cut Your Chills," and they performed it at over fifty different schools. Sir Mix-A-Lot wrote the lyrics, and Sir Wes performed the rap.

1982

ORIGINAL RAPPIN' THREE

Back in 1981, Jeremy Beckwith rapped with Eddie "Sugar Bear" Wells, who had given Beckwith the nickname "Sweet J." But by 1982, Beckwith had stopped hanging out with Sugar Bear as much, now that Bear was busy with the increasingly popular Emerald Street Boys trio.

Beckwith went out on his own as a solo rapper named Sweet J for a while. He would battle kids in Rainier Beach and also in the halls at Franklin High School. Meanwhile, Rcurtis Jamerson had become the new de facto Sweet J in Emerald Street Boys. Not surprisingly, Beckwith developed a minor beef with Jamerson, mostly over the use of the name Sweet J.

This led to some problems. According to Beckwith, he had silkscreened a jacket with the name Sweet J on the back and an image of a stylized microphone, and he didn't want to get rid of it. Beckwith let a girlfriend borrow the jacket, and she was wearing it out one day. A guy who had a beef with Jamerson saw the name Sweet J on the back, and he mistakenly thought that she was a friend of Jamerson. The guy confronted her and told her to take the jacket off. She was confused until she explained that she didn't even know Jamerson. This Sweet J was Jeremy Beckwith, she told the guy.

Later, as Jamerson recalls, he had a confrontation with Beckwith in front of the downtown Musicland on Third Avenue. The two exchanged words and almost had a fight. Beckwith realized the name wasn't worth fighting over, and soon after this, he changed his rap name to "J.B."

J.B. next joined a group called the Original Rappin' Three, which included J.B., Thomas "Skeee" Washington and another Thomas who went by the nickname "Colonel Click." J.B. laughs at the coincidence, "It was me and the Thomases."

In a 2020 interview, Skeee remembered, "We used to go to Lateef's, everybody was there, all the prime players from back in the day, [MC] 3-D, [Ronnie] Beasley, Silver Chain Gang, we was all there and we was doing it big. Seattle had a scene back in the early eighties." Eventually, Original Rappin' Three broke up, and the members went their separate ways.

J.B. formed a new clique called Q Boys, who took their name from the "Q" in *Gentleman's Quarterly* magazine. The Q Boys included J.B., Daryl "Smurf" Murphy, Glen Ferguson, Aaron Nellams and a DJ named Dale Yamashita. They were not a rap group; instead, they were more like a house party crew. Q Boys would throw big parties, with b-boys and b-girls coming from all over the city. A house at Twenty-Fifth Avenue and Lane Street was a popular spot, and near the intersection of Thirty-First Avenue and Howell Street was another good one. J.B. remembers Sugar Bear pulling up to one memorable party at Forty-Eighth Avenue and Kenyon Street in a clean-looking Ford.

Q Boys had a strategy for their house parties to maintain the right balance of guys and girls. According to J.B., they would station a half-dozen people to congregate right by the door, so if some guys were trying to come in, the doorman could just point to the crowded hallway and say, "Sorry, the party is too full." But if it was some girls, the doorman would just let them in, and the decoy crowd would magically clear the entryway to the house.

Not every gig was a success. J.B. remembers arranging a DJ event in Tacoma at the Al Davies Boys and Girls Club. It was an afterparty for the state track meet in the Tacoma Dome. Q Boys got all set up and started playing hip hop and dance music. But soon, a bunch of tough-looking guys came in and surrounded the DJ. They made it clear that Q Boys weren't welcome in Tacoma and that they better get the hell out of there. J.B. and the rest of the Q Boys took their advice, and they scrambled to collect the audio gear, escaping safely back to Seattle.

SOUTHSIDE THREE

Bobby "MC 3-D" Stills went to O'Dea High School in Seattle as a freshman in 1981. He would ride the Metro route no. 7 and rap in the back of the bus. Many people remember MC 3-D being a prolific rapper from the very beginning, and he was also known as one of the freshest-dressed b-boys in Seattle.

As MC 3-D got more into rap music, he wanted to record a song he had written called "Tape Deck Pimp." He recalls being assisted by his friend Scottie Pettison, who was a bit of an electronics whiz. Pettison had learned that he could string four cassette decks together into a quadrophonic receiver. That way, Pettison could combine multiple tapes into a single blended mixdown.

At some point after Q Boys broke up, J.B. ran into MC 3-D in hip hop circles, and the two clicked. They were both heavily involved with the hip hop lifestyle, and they became a crew.

MC 3-D then introduced J.B. to a friend of his named Eddie "Sunshine" Ausler, who had moved to Seattle from Kansas City, Missouri. Sunshine liked boxing, and several of his siblings were also boxers. He came from a religious family, and MC 3-D remembers it was always time-consuming to go pick him up, because Sunshine's mother would force them to sit and listen to her talk about the Bible.

Sunshine, MC 3-D and J.B. teamed up and named themselves "Southside Three." They did some shows together and participated in rap battles.

(*Left to right*) Jeremy "J.B." Beckwith, Aaron Nellams (Q Boys) and Bobby "MC 3-D" Stills. *Photograph courtesy of Bobby Stills.*

According to J.B., Sunshine didn't write his own raps, but he had a good stage presence and was an excellent dancer.

At one battle between Southside Three and Emerald Street Boys at Campion Towers, MC 3-D almost got Southside Three into big trouble. MC 3-D would put the taped intros together using audio gear in his small bedroom studio. Well, for this battle, MC 3-D had incorporated some Funkadelic and other spacey records. The problem was that Emerald Street Boys had been using the same intro and were already known for it. So, when the audio started playing during the battle, it almost led to a fight. Emerald Street Boys rushed the stage calling foul and demanded that Southside Three quit biting their sound.

Southside Three had a song called "Royalty." The lyrics included the line, "We're the disco kings, with diamond rings, when we start to sing, ladies we bring." Like many songs of this era, it was rapped to an instrumental B-side. In this case, the instrumental was "That's the Joint" by Funky 4 + 1. Eventually, they stopped hanging out and the group dissolved. Around this time, MC 3-D gravitated toward a celebrated local rap group called West Coast Funk Brigade.

WEST COAST FUNK BRIGADE

Ronnie "Duke of Double Rock" Beasley grew up in Seattle and attended three different high schools: Garfield, Nathan Hale and Ingraham. He got into rap very early and called himself "Ronnie B." His main accessory was his big double-cassette boombox, which he carried everywhere. He was early friends with Sugar Bear from Emerald Street Boys, and he hung out with that group from time to time.

Eric "Deputy Rhyme" Gordon grew up in Seattle and attended Leschi Elementary. He became friends with a student named Roy Jackson, and both of them were into music. They were fascinated by the sounds of "Rapper's Delight," so they made up rap names for themselves. Jackson became "Royal Rap," and Gordon became "Deputy Rhyme." They never really named their group, and Deputy Rhyme remembers that the two never actually recorded any songs either.

Deputy Rhyme moved from Seattle to San Diego for about a year while he was in high school. While in San Diego, he was classmates with Faizon Love, who would go on to become a famous comedian. Deputy Rhyme also remembers hanging out at the Stratus Club, a famous San Diego nightclub. "We used to jones on other kids all the time," recalls Deputy. *Jones* was another word for "capping" or "ranking."

By 1981, Deputy Rhyme was back in Seattle, and he rode the school bus every day with Beasley. One day, Beasley was freestyling for fun, putting rhymes together one after the other. Deputy Rhyme heard the rapping and was excited. "I rap, too," he told Beasley, and then Deputy started saying some rhymes. Beasley was amazed at Deputy's flow and delivery. "He was off the hook," recalls Beasley. The two teamed up to form a new rap duo called West Coast Funk Brigade. Desiring a more unique stage name, Beasley changed his handle from Ronnie B. to "Duke of Double Rock."

Deputy Rhyme is quick to emphasize why they chose their group name. "We were the first ones out here representing Seattle and the West Coast," he explains. It was important for them to put "West Coast" in the name to show pride in where they were from.

Both Duke of Double Rock and Deputy Rhyme were obsessed with rap music. One day, Double Rock's friend Kevin Austin told him about a group from West Seattle called Jam Delight. Double Rock went to see them perform, and he was very impressed. Jam Delight inspired him to keep working hard in the rap game.

Soon, West Coast Funk Brigade had a repertoire of songs they could perform live. According to Deputy Rhyme, the first track he remembers was called "Little Red Rock 'Em Good." A second song was called "Freaky, Freaky." They also wrote a cut called "The Freeze," which included lines like, "The temperature's cold, it's twenty below, you might get a chill, you might get cold." Both members of West Coast Funk Brigade recall performing at shows with Emerald Street Boys and Emerald Street Girls.

West Coast Funk Brigade were prolific, and they often tailored their lyrics to fit the specific event where they would be rapping. If they played a Halloween show, they would write a rap that day and then perform it that night at the party. When asked how many songs they had, Double Rock remembers it was "more than ten."

According to Deputy Rhyme, he would often see Bobby "MC 3-D" Stills at parties and rhyme battles. Deputy Rhyme brought MC 3-D to Double Rock, and 3-D did a rap tryout for the two of them. MC 3-D's verses were so good that he was allowed to join the group, and he performed with West Coast Funk Brigade at some of their shows.

They received an honorable mention for their performance at the April 1982 All-City rap-off. In a write-up about the event, the group's full name,

West Coast Funk Brigade Fusion Funkateers, was used. As Deputy Rhyme remembers it, "We were lyrically ahead of our time." They tried to make their rhymes "intricate like Tetris." He recalls the tension between all the early '80s Seattle rap groups who were in heated competition for the number one spot.

But that highest honor was elusive for many Seattle rappers. Thanks in part to the efforts of SNECO, Emerald Street Boys had cracked the code to local stardom. Now everyone else wanted that top spot, too. Deputy describes Emerald Street Boys at the time as "Hammer before there was Hammer," due to the fancy costumes and dance routines that comprised their live shows.

BARON VON SCRATCH

Jerome "Baron Von Scratch" Gibson's family moved to the Seattle area in 1978, and he went to Mercer Middle School. At Mercer, he watched the development of bopping culture as it grew in popularity. Gibson wasn't into bopping, but he soon met a few friends who were. One of his fellow Mercer students was Michael "Space Cowboy" McDonald. Gibson entered Rainier Beach High School a few years later.

The famous hip hopper and cap rapper Eric "Puppet" Grant gave Gibson his first turntables. Puppet was a very early bopper from the north end of Seattle who turned to rapping and DJing. As a bopper and a DJ who was dialed in to the New York scene, he would often have tapes of shows by Mr. Magic on WBLS or Red Alert on WRKS. As Gibson recalls, Puppet would bring back all the hot records from out of state that weren't yet available in local stores. Gibson remembers Puppet played an early Blowfly rap song for him, and he was also the first to have Fatback Band's 1979 hit "King Tim III," which came out several months before "Rapper's Delight."

Puppet once DJed a very successful party at the local YWCA. He was decked out in battery-powered glasses called Zany Zappers that lit up around the frames. The crowd was dancing, as Gibson remembers, and Puppet mixed Blondie's "Rapture" into "The Adventures of Grandmaster Flash on the Wheels of Steel." A lightbulb flashed over Gibson's head, and he knew he wanted to do this new hip hop thing for real.

In addition to hanging out with Puppet, Gibson also kicked it with Space Cowboy. They would meet at Lateef's. Sometimes, at Lateef's, there would be a spontaneous Burger King versus McDonald's rap contest. The battlers would still have their uniforms on, having come straight from their shifts. Three or four McDonald's employees would trade rhymes with employees who worked at Burger King.

Speaking of Burger King, one of Gibson's early jobs was cleaning the grease traps at Burger King during the graveyard shift. The manager would lock the workers in at night and then come in the next morning to let them out. Gibson also cleaned offices at Xerox for a measly $3.35 per hour. He had to do many odd jobs to have money for DJ equipment and blank tapes.

When money was really tight, he could resort to stealing the all-day pass books from an unattended Metro bus. Sometimes, the drivers would park and leave the bus door open. The passes were kept right by the door, and if he was quick, Gibson could snatch a whole bunch of passes and then later sell them for cash at a video game arcade near his house.

Gibson remembers the first time he met Anthony "Sir Mix-A-Lot" Ray, who lived just a few blocks down South Henderson Street. Gibson was walking with his crew through Lakeshore Village apartments, and one of them carried a loud box playing an original mixtape. In addition to the boombox, Gibson always had his bright blue Pan-Am shoulder bag with his mixtapes for sale inside. Ray stuck his head out of his apartment window to ask what the music was, and they became acquainted. From that point forward, Gibson and his crew knew that they could knock on the window if they wanted to get in touch with Ray.

They started hanging out regularly, and they both enjoyed watching a Hanna Barbera cartoon called *Wacky Races* on Saturday mornings. One of the *Wacky Races* characters named Red Max was modeled after real-life World War I pilot "The Red Baron." Another *Wacky Races* character named Dick Dastardly had a brother named "Dread Baron," who appeared in a different Hanna Barbera cartoon called *Laff-a-Lympics*. Gibson remembers vividly that while watching one of those two programs, he and Ray chose their performance names. He doesn't remember which show they were watching, but interestingly, episode 14A of *Wacky Races*, titled "Speeding for Smogland," features a Hollywood set where they are filming a King Arthur and the Knights of the Round Table movie. Inspired by these classic cartoons, Gibson chose "Baron Von Scratch" as his name, while Ray, who had been calling himself Spaceman, chose "Sir Mix-A-Lot."

Sir Mix-A-Lot recalls Baron Von Scratch with respect: "What I liked about him, he was pure art. He wasn't one of these guys sitting around waiting for

Anthony "Sir Mix-A-Lot" Ray (*left*) and Jerome "Baron Von Scratch" Gibson (*right*). *Photograph courtesy of Pete Kuhns, appeared in* The Rocket *in May 1985.*

the check." Mix-A-Lot and Baron Von Scratch sparked creativity in each other, and they became a battle duo. Mix-A-Lot had the programming skills and all the drum machines. Baron was more of a DJ than a programmer, so they each had their skillsets. Baron remembers once trying to popularize the slow backspin reverse beat, but people didn't appreciate how cool the whooshing backward beat sounded.

When Run DMC's "Hard Times" single came out in 1983, Baron and Mix-A-Lot listened to it over and over. Baron was excited and wanted to imitate the group, but as he recalls, Mix-A-Lot was more inclined to make fun of it. Regardless, they both were strongly influenced by the new sound. According to Baron, the two of them made some songs that mocked the simple cadences of Run DMC.

Baron Von Scratch remembers an early one-on-one battle versus Mix-A-Lot they did just for practice. Mix-A-Lot pulled out "Cosmic Cars," by Cybotron, and started cutting it. Baron wasn't familiar with the song yet, and it blew his mind. He admits that he had to concede the battle to Mix. Around the same time, they had another jam session. Baron played "I.O.U." by Freeez in that matchup, and Mix-A-Lot had Awesome Foursome and

Nairobi's "Funky Soul Makossa." They went back and forth battling, cutting and scratching. It wasn't really about who was winning; instead, it was more about musical experimentation and having fun.

A lot of hip hop fans would congregate in Seward Park on Lake Washington, or The Arboretum, which is a giant 230-acre mixed-use city park. Some would have noise battles between car systems or boombox against boombox to see whose was the loudest. Baron decided to win one of these park battles with a daring technical plan. He brought his boombox and then hooked it up to an Alpine brand car amplifier to boost the sound. Because the amp was way too powerful for the boombox, the noise was loud and thundering, a total success.

Baron Von Scratch wanted to be able to scratch his own name, which was the dream of any hip hop DJ. As it turned out, The Pacific Science Center featured an exhibit where you could go in and make your own record. You could say something, and then it would be cut into a small record which you could bring home. There was also an exhibit at The Science Center that made your voice sound like a robot. Baron couldn't believe how cool the technology was.

When it came to DJing and production, Baron was very proud of his mixtapes, including one called *Mega Mix III* and another titled *Roxanne's Remix*. He remembers his first four-track deck was a Fostex X-15. The first song he released as a rapper was called "Chrome Dome Jerome," but he's not sure of the exact recording date.

SIR LOVER THE MC

Ronnie "Sir Lover the MC" Jones shared a room with his brother growing up and often set the radio to KYAC at night as they were going to bed. One night, Jones heard "Rapper's Delight," and his ears immediately perked up. His brother also noticed, and they both sat up in bed and listened to the sounds of The Sugarhill Gang. Just like Sweet J from Emerald Street Boys and many others, Jones will never forget hearing rap for the first time and thinking how strange it sounded to his young ears.

Jones attended Roosevelt High School at first but transferred to Lindbergh in Renton before going back to Roosevelt. He also attended Marshall and Sharples, which were alternative high schools for students who were not fitting in at the regular high schools. Jones remembers that Sharples sometimes felt like the school portrayed in the film *Lean on Me*: "You could get in a fight at school and then go to your next class as if nothing had happened," he recalls.

During his high school years, Jones would often go to parties at Donnie Mitchell's house, whose family lived at Twenty-First Avenue and Union Street. A young man named Jeff Cunningham lived near the Mitchell family, and at one of these parties, Jones was introduced to Cunningham. The two became a rap duo, The Sir Lovers. They chose this name after watching *To Sir, with Love*, which features a strong performance by actor Sidney Poitier.

The Sir Lovers really weren't very serious as far as rap was concerned. Cunningham called himself Sir Lover no. 1, and Jones called himself Sir Lover no. 2, but they never put any complete songs together. Cunningham wasn't as motivated as Jones, and eventually, The Sir Lovers broke up for lack of energy. Jones liked the name Sir Lover, so he continued using the name after leaving the group. He added "the MC" to make the name sound more complete. His hero at the time was Kool Moe Dee from New York.

Sir Lover the MC's parents were intent on giving him a good education, so they kept encyclopedias in the home for him to read. He bought a rhyming dictionary and would study it to get the best words for his battles. Sir Lover also scoured the current events section of the daily newspaper for fresh topics. All of these different sources of information combined to give him a major edge over lazy MCs who just said the same old stuff.

As time went on, Sir Lover the MC became more experienced and learned how to maximize the effect of his rhymes. If Sir Mix-A-Lot was DJing a party at the Boys and Girls Club, there was an extremely good chance that Mix would let up-and-coming rappers line up after the show and rap to a beat. Sir Lover would let all the hotheads go first, and then he would wait to be the last MC to rock the mic. It worked, because his rhymes were the last things in people's minds after each showcase. All the guys who had pushed to the front of the line were forgotten.

Sir Lover the MC got a part-time internship at a local record store called Dirt Cheap Records and Tapes. The store at Twenty-Second Avenue and Union Street was a neighborhood fixture that was owned by J.W. Johnson, who had moved to Seattle from Chicago. Every day, he would park his classic automobile out in front of the store. Johnson saw that there was money in video games, too, so he added an arcade above the Union Street store. Eventually, Johnson opened a second Dirt Cheap location on Holly Street and then a third shop in the Tacoma area.

In fact, professor and author Dr. Daudi Abe was an early Dirt Cheap customer way back in 1979. In a 2006 piece in *The Stranger*, Dr. Abe remembered buying his first rap record. "My pops took me to Dirt Cheap Records, which used to be right behind Richlen's gas station," he wrote. "Not having any idea of what I wanted to get, I wandered around the store until I happened to see a twelve-inch jacket with a swirling, multicolored logo that reminded me of candy." The record, of course, was "Rapper's Delight," by The Sugarhill Gang.

ALL CITY BATTLE OF THE RAPPERS

In March 1982, there was a giant rap battle at Empire Plaza. *The Rocket*'s listing promised a good show: "Battle of the Rappers, Fri. 3/12 at the Empire Plaza. 820 Empire Way S. Our faves, Emerald Street Boys and other local rappers defend their turf against fast-talking New Yorkers."

Michael "Mellow Mike" Thomas (from Cosmic Crew) was declared the winner, according to the "Lip Service" column in the April issue of *The Rocket*. "Mellow Mike narrowly edged out Snap Crackle Pop to take top honors in the rapper's competition held at the Empire Plaza in mid-March," reported the paper. Snap Crackle Pop were an early trio composed of Anthony Steward (Snap), Jay Nelson (Crackle) and Brian Nelson (Pop). Emerald Street Boys were not competing, but their performance at the event "provided more rappertainment when the competition was over."

The April 1982 edition of *The Rocket* also ran a listing for the follow-up battle that was to occur on April 9. This second All City contest was held at Campion Tower on the Seattle University campus. Judging the rap-off was a panel including writer Robert Newman from *The Rocket*. The night began with a disco at 9:00 p.m., and then the competition was at 11:00 p.m. After the battle, the music continued until 2:00 a.m.

In May, the paper covered the battle, writing, "The second city-wide rap off on April 9 at Campion Towers was a big success." The piece went on, "Organized by Victor Clark and Starcity Productions, the contest was won by the Wonder Twins [featuring the Casanova Kid and Twinkle B], with the Groovy Gangster Girls coming in a close second." According to the article, "Special mention goes to the West Coast Funk Brigade Fusion Funkateers, who had a great rap. Judges included Joe Boot, owner of Rainier Music Menu, Angela Barnes, and *The Rocket*'s Bob Newman."

Proving that April 9, 1982, was a significant date for Seattle rap, *The Rocket*'s May piece also mentioned, "That same night [April 9], Emerald Street Boys helped inaugurate the Dragon Palace's new music format with Memory and 3 Swimmers."

These two rap battles paved the way for another rhyme competition. In July 1982, an announcement ran in *The Facts*: "DJ Black Nasty and G.P.I. will hold a teen dance rap-off July 29th at the beautiful Lateef's on Rainier Avenue South."

"ULTRA GROOVE"

Tony Benton went to Seattle's Franklin High School, and he played in a band called Crystal Clear. The bassist had a clear electric bass guitar, and when he went away to the army, he gave the see-through bass to Benton. Soon, Benton was the frontman of an R&B group called Teleclere.

According to a piece by Robert Newman in *The Rocket*, Teleclere came together near the end of 1981. T.C. Wilson played drums and percussion, while Kyle McKinney handled guitar and vocals. In that article, Benton listed a few musical influences, including Stevie Wonder, Rufus & Chaka Khan and Parliament.

T.C. Wilson (*left*) and Tony Benton (*right*). *Photograph courtesy of Mark Sullo, appeared in* The Rocket *in September 1983.*

At their live shows that year, they performed cover versions of popular songs, including "Forget Me Nots," by Patrice Rushen; "Whip It," by Devo; and "Early in the Morning," by The Gap Band. Benton explained to Newman, "We have a lot of confidence in our own material….When we do covers we want to play the top 40 stuff so it's unique."

In 1982, Teleclere wrote more songs, and they released a seven-inch single called "Fantasy Love" on Benton's newly minted Telemusic record label. "Fantasy Love" is a R&B love song including vocals by M. Johnson. For Benton, it was very important for him to be involved in every step of the record manufacturing process. Having an independent record label was a huge accomplishment, but he recalls that it took a lot of work.

Teleclere was experimenting with many different musical styles. On the B-side of "Fantasy Love" was a track called "Ultra Groove." Unlike the A-side, "Ultra Groove" had proto-rap verses that occurred near the beginning and end of the track. A robotic effect on the vocals made the words swim and vibrate as they were rapped.

Excerpt:

Ultra Groove is going through my feet
This is a groove to make you move to the beat
Teleclere here with the funky sound
To make your party get on down
Not too high and not too low
Ultra Groove is in Steree-eree-o

Give it a chance you old fool
Cause this tune here is Ultra Groove

© 1982 Teleclere

The rap vibe in "Ultra Groove" was unmistakable. There was a chant at the end of "Ultra Groove" that was very hip hop–inspired as well. "Move your feet, clap your hands, everybody dance," repeated over and over, and it's easy to imagine a crowd rapping along with the group at a live performance of the song. The "Fantasy Love" single was available to purchase at Musicland on Third Avenue and Pike Street and other Seattle music shops.

This was the second vinyl record from Seattle that had raps on it, but it was really the first to be connected to the voice of hip hop culture in New York. "I'm Little Ray Rapper" was clever and innovative, but its DNA traced back to lighthearted comedy albums rather than the real rap attitude of East Coast city streets. The spacey raps in "Ultra Groove" hinted at a less rehearsed and more freestyle approach to music. Benton had felt the pulse of his generation, and he was responding to it in a major way. He embraced rap instead of rejecting it.

BLACK COMMUNITY FESTIVAL

A citywide, multi-community festival called Seafair was first held in Seattle in 1950. According to History Link, although Seafair reached out to international communities, it was still seen as primarily for white residents. In 1952, a Black businessman named Russell Gideon started his own festival for the city's Black community. It was informally called the East Madison Mardi Gras, as reported in *The Seattle Post Intelligencer*. According to historian Peter Blecha, the annual event took the name Black Community Festival in the late 1960s.

Emerald Street Boys dominated a Black Community Festival rap contest in the summer of 1982. They performed in matching white shirts and slacks, with Panama hats and tan shoes. They were photographed at the event during the awarding of the winners' trophy. In one image, the host of the event, DJ Black Nasty, is seen speaking into a microphone. Emerald Street Boys and Emerald Street Girls are both onstage as Captain Crunch holds the trophy. After Emerald Street Boys left the stage, someone also took a historic snapshot of the trio standing proudly in front of a red curtain.

The Rocket mentioned the '82 festival in its "Funk" column. "The Emerald Street Boys won the Black Community Festival Rap-Off, but the very live Emerald Street Girls stole the show," reported the paper. Then the writer described the clothes worn by Emerald Street Girls: "Angel Face and Lady Di appeared in very bad red and black new wave mini-skirts complete with wraparound sunglasses. Rapping to the B-side of The Fearless Four's 'It's Magic,' the [Emerald Street] Girls were definitely too hot to handle too cool to freeze."

In 1983, there was a big marketing push to promote the festival, especially in *The Facts* newspaper, which wrote about the plans early that year. "According to the Pacific Northwest Black Community Festival Association, a newly created organization, the Community Festival will be a joyous celebration of the Pacific Northwest Black experience, in every aspect of life," the paper announced.

Before the musical portion of the event, there was a parade that featured many prominent local figures and many vintage antique cars, too. A battle of the bands was also part of the lineup. Thousands of people gathered in the crowd to see the performances.

Garfield High School student Mike Clark, who had listened to Frostmaster Chill and Mellow Mike rap in art class back in 1981, distinctly remembers taking the no. 48 Metro bus to the festival. As Clark recounted in 2024

(*Left to right*) Emerald Street Boys, Emerald Street Girls and DJ Black Nasty at the Black Community Festival 1982. *Photograph courtesy of Dr. James Croone.*

for the As Many Weirdos as Possible photographic history project, "Gary [Jam] and I were talking on the phone, and he told me to come to the Black Community Festival at Judkins Park the next day to see them perform." Clark recalled that after witnessing Jam Delight and other local rap stars that day, he decided that he was going to get a job in the music business.

Even though they had auditioned for the festival, Silver Chain Gang were not on the bill. Finally, the festival was over, and the crowd was leaving because the marquee act, Exposure, was done playing. Victor "DJ

Starchild" Clark was the host, and he announced that the entertainment was concluded. But suddenly, there was a commotion. A friend of the Silver Chain Gang crew named Doug was there with his mom, and according to DJ Lee, all of a sudden, Doug's mother was loudly advocating to let Silver Chain Gang perform. Somehow, she was able to convince Starchild to let Silver Chain Gang come onstage and rap while everyone left Judkins Park, the festival's location.

The Silver Chain Gang started with a song they had written called "Boys Can Rock," which used "Theme from *Shaft*" as an intro. While all the members of Silver Chain Gang hid backstage, DJ Lee went up and set the needle on the *Shaft* record. As the instantly recognizable music played, the Silver Chain Gang members each jumped out into view, one person at a time. Soon, they were all on stage rocking the microphones.

When the departing crowd heard the *Shaft* theme and then the rapping, many started to turn around and then go back to the stage to hear what was going on. As Duke of Earl remembered, "Half the crowd was leaving, and the other half was moving back toward the stage." It was chaos. After Silver Chain Gang had performed all their rehearsed material, DJ Lee and Doug joined them onstage for an impromptu live freestyle with scratching and cutting. DJ Lee remembers that after the show, people were literally asking for their autographs.

THE ROCKET

The Rocket was a Seattle newspaper dedicated to local music, and it did an excellent job chronicling the first generation of Seattle rap. In a 1982 piece called "Armory Wrap Up," Robert Newman wrote a long description of Emerald Street Boys early in their career. An all-city rap-off that spring at Campion Towers was judged by Newman, as reported in a piece in *The Rocket* that referred to him as "Big Bob Newman." October 1982 saw a Newman article about Teleclere, whose album *Affection/Defection* he also reviewed at the time of its release. "Last year Teleclere released one of the best singles I've ever heard from the Seattle area," he wrote, referring to "Fantasy Love."

From 1983 to 1986, Newman was the editor at *The Rocket*. The paper's coverage of rap music during these years continued to be impressive. There were full-page stories about Afrika Bambaataa, Grandmaster Flash and Treacherous Three. Especially during 1983, the paper spent lots of coverage on Emerald Street Boys. The January 1983 issue contained a list of the "Seattle Top Ten Exciting Bands" from 1982, with Emerald Street Boys sitting pretty at number one.

One of Newman's favorite experiences was walking along with Emerald Street Boys in the Seafair Torchlight Parade, which was a major annual event in downtown Seattle. As Newman was quoted in the book *Emerald Street: A History of Seattle Hip Hop*, "[Emerald Street Boys] danced and performed along the parade route, attracting a giant crowd of adoring teens." His recollection really painted a picture: "Their soundtrack consisted of me carrying a giant boombox and playing the instrumental side of 'The Message' over and over."

Another prolific rap writer at *The Rocket* was "Shockmaster" Glen Boyd. He graduated from West Seattle High School in 1974 and developed an early passion for music. In 1980, he got a job working in Lakewood at Penny Lane Records. His name appeared in *The Rocket* starting in 1982. He also published an opinion piece in *Billboard* magazine, in which he argued in favor

Members of *The Rocket* staff in 1981. *Photograph courtesy of Mark Sullo, appeared in* The Rocket *in October 1981.*

of putting Black artists' videos on MTV. At the time of Boyd's editorial, the cable music channel was airing only videos from white artists.

Boyd became a local proponent of what was still called "funk" music at *The Rocket*. For example, in January 1984, Boyd penned a recap of the ten best funk songs from the previous year. On that list, Boyd included Run DMC's "It's Like That"; "Jam on Revenge," by Newcleus; and Herbie Hancock's innovative song "Rockit." "New York's 'hip hop' sound, with its beat boxes and break dancing, became a nationwide phenomenon [in 1983], through small labels like Tommy Boy, and artists like Soul Sonic Force, Planet Patrol, and Spyder D," he wrote.

Music historian Charles R. Cross was editor at the *UW Daily* in 1979 and then joined *The Rocket* in 1981 as a contributing writer. Cross especially recalls Robert Newman as a proponent of hip hop music at the paper in those days. "He was way ahead of the game on rap," explains Cross, "and his enthusiasm helped many in Seattle discover the genre."

Cross dedicated himself to music journalism, and he became editor of *The Rocket* when Newman left in the fall of 1986. Regarding the first generation of rap, Cross was a fan. "Initially I loved the first rap I heard, as I'd identify politically as a socialist, and it felt like both a musical and political movement." As a jukebox collector, he always made sure to have "The Message" by Grandmaster Flash as one of the 45s available to choose.

But like many listeners, Cross was sad to see those early messages of hope turned into callousness and greed. "As rap became more gangsta, and thematically moved away from what I felt was the political moment, I was less interested," he says.

Cross remembers the early '80s as an exciting time to be in Seattle. "At some of the dance clubs in Seattle, like Tugs and the Vogue, rap songs were certainly played alongside new wave in the early eighties." Similar to the observations of DJ Mike Joyce, Cross's recollections are that "there wasn't a divide between rap and punk or new wave at the time: all of it was edgy."

Before Sub Pop was an internationally successful record label, it was a monthly column in *The Rocket* written by Bruce Pavitt. The column was devoted to a wide variety of musical styles and immediately became a very early source for Seattle readers to learn about new and exciting rap music tracks. In fact, the very first "Sub Pop" column in April 1983 included write-ups of "Play at Your Own Risk," by Planet Patrol, and "Let's Get Small," by Trouble Funk. "I didn't write about the local stuff," Pavitt explains.

Some other examples of "Sub Pop" rap reviews from 1983 were of Treacherous Three's "Action" in May, Afrika Bambaataa's "Looking for the Perfect Beat" and Grandmaster Flash's "NY, NY" in June and Disco 3 "Reality" in December. These "Sub Pop" columns gave credibility to rap music and brought these artists to the attention of readers all over Seattle.

In October 1983, Pavitt devoted the entire "Sub Pop" column to "Black/Funk/Rap" music. Looking back, Pavitt remembers one event that gave him an indication of rap's nascent power. "I was DJing an all ages punk club [Metropolis] in Pioneer Square in the summer of '83," recalls Pavitt. "I dropped 'It's Like That' [DMC] and the crowd went off. I believe that track represented a turning point of sorts, as it was being heard all over Seattle. DMC hit hard with that single (great flipside too, with Sucker MC's)."

Pavitt had a personal interest in hip hop that coexisted alongside his work as a rock journalist. "I remember being impressed by the Schooly D record in '85," he recalls, "which, interestingly, was being distributed by Rough Trade, an iconic punk/indie distributor." In the early '80s, especially in the pages of *The Rocket*, there was a sense that all types of music could coexist together, rap included. Seattle was a true musical utopia for many of the residents.

1983

"CHRISTMAS RAP"

SNECO included Emerald Street Boys in many of their theatrical productions, including the *Entertainment Live* series. One performance in the summer of 1983 was described in *The Facts* newspaper. "Based on *Saturday Night Live*–styled scenes and comedy sketches, interwoven with hard-hitting vocal and musical numbers, as well as rappers, a comedian, and a magician, *It's Entertainment Live* offers a panoramic view of Seattle's best, doing what they do best," wrote the paper.

In the February 1983 issue of *Trouser Press* magazine, Emerald Street Boys were mentioned in an article about Seattle music. It was a big deal to get a write up in a New York–based rock-and-roll magazine, and the piece helped the group gain notability. "Emerald Street Boys recently won the Black Community All City Rap-Off with 'The Message' and a new wave rap," announced the article. It continued, "They faced stiff competition from The Emerald Street Girls and the Silver Chain Gang."

May 27, 1983, was another big day for Emerald Street Boys. They got top placement in *The Seattle Post Intelligencer*'s "What's Happening" section of the paper. "Rappin' And Poppin' with the Emerald Street Boys and Girls," ran the headline. The piece was accompanied by a photograph of the group smiling for the camera. "Tonight, On the Boards presents a Memorial Day weekend celebration featuring rap music by the Emerald Street Boys and the Emerald Street Girls," read the listing.

Starcity Entertainment Co.

proudly presents

After Rick James Affair

Featuring Seattle Rap Sensations

The Emerald Street Boys

and Special Guest Appearances by

JAM-DELIGHT

Place: Tacoma Bicentennial Pavilion
1313 Market, Downtown Tacoma
Date: November 15, 1983
Time: 11:00 p.m.
Price: $5.00/$4.00 with Rick James Ticket stub
Advanced tickets at T.J.'s Men Shop & the Tacoma Bicentennial Pavilion

More Info: Seattle 329-4235 Tacoma 597-7234

A poster for a Starcity Entertainment party, November 15, 1983. The poster includes a photograph by Kristine Larsen. *Poster courtesy of Ryan Croone, photograph by author.*

"Christmas Rap." © *1983 Telemusic Productions, scan by author.*

Tony Benton of Teleclere wanted to release a hip hop–themed Christmas record, and he first approached Silver Chain Gang. According to Duke of Earl, Silver Chain Gang submitted a demo tape to Benton of something they had written. But Benton listened to it and decided that it wasn't what he had in mind, so he kept searching.

Benton next reached out to Emerald Street Boys and subsequently made a deal with Sugar Bear's mother, Carol Wells, who was the group's business manager. Although Bembry expressed some reservations, he and Sneed eventually agreed to go ahead with the deal. According to Bembry, he felt that a holiday record was not the best way to debut a single for the group. Near the end of 1983, *The Facts* ran a piece about Emerald Street Boys. "Emerald Street Boys Will Soon Wrap on Wax," ran the headline above the article by writer Kelvin James.

"The Emerald Street Boys, a longtime favorite Seattle act, with their unique style of rapping and dancing, have signed a recording contract with Telemusic Productions, Seattle's Black-owned record production and manufacturing company," announced the piece. Lonnie Mitchell from Telemusic said, "I believe the Emerald Street Boys are peerless in the Northwest for what they do." The article mentioned that the group expected to be finished with their single by December 1983.

Tony Benton brought Emerald Street Boys to Woodmont Beach Studio and recorded two tracks, "Christmas Rap" and "The Move." Sweet J remembers being starstruck: "I had heard about studios, and here I was inside one for the first time." One of the studio engineers was seeing peaks from the microphone and approached the group. He told them they couldn't say the Ps and Ts like they usually did because the air was popping the mic. As Sweet J recalls, they would have to say "bresents" instead of "presents."

Excellent vocals were provided by singer Cassandra Callier, and Teleclere played the backing musical track. The three rappers each took turns delivering alternating lines in the verses. The song began with all three of them introducing themselves one by one. Later in the track, the melody for "Rudolph the Red Nosed Reindeer" was incorporated into a verse.

Excerpt:

Merry Christmas from C-C
Girl I'll wait for you up under the tree
What you want for Christmas well just move and see
So my gift to you is to rock a party
Merry Christmas from Sugar Bear
No batteries, accessories, I'm not nothing you wear
Show me to your friends you won't want to share
Cause I'm the toy that brings you joy you can't compare
Merry Christmas from Sweet J
I'll rock with might all though the night, girl you wanna play
We're the baby dolls and we want to say
We're gonna rock your Christmas in a different way

Check out the way we rock this, yes the smooth MCs
And if you ever saw us, we're sure you'll all agree
All of the other rappers know that they can't compare
With the mighty Captain, Sweet J, and Sugar Bear

Like snow on the ground and you forgot your glove
Like wintertime and you fell in love
With a cute little bear that was all alone
You just couldn't help it, you carried him home
You sat him by the tree and by your surprise
That very night he came alive

Merry Christmas to our hometown, Seattle
If you can hear it then it's going around
Merry Christmas to our ladies
Marline, Lynette, and of course Jackie

© 1983 Emerald Street Boys

Accompanying "Christmas Rap" was "The Move," a very solid rap cut that proved the group had more in their verbal toolboxes. Sugar Bear wrote a rhyme about his girlfriend Marline Russell and included it in the track. Careful listeners will know that Russell had also been recognized in "Christmas Rap." All three MCs dropped innovative raps on "The Move," which reminded all contenders that Emerald Street Boys wore the crown in Seattle.

Excerpt:

The Sugar Bear, the myth and the fable
I'm the mixer magician with the two turntables
Captain Crunch you know that's me
Rocking to the rhythm to the T-O-P
The mellow man, the third MC of the crew
You best believe Sweet J will start rocking you

Extra, extra, read all about it
It's a new discovery and don't you dare doubt it

About two years back on the rapping scene
I met a fly girl by the name of Marline
I took a good look, the girl was so fine
I said c'mon baby won't you be mine
She said Sugar Bear, I heard about you
And all the heartbreaking that you do
Just telling you now it just couldn't be
Because one broken heart is too many for me
I said this time around I'll make things right
We'll make love through the night cause Sugar Bear's a delight
Bring forth all your dreams, you and I king and queen
Together forever Sugar Bear and Marline

© 1983 Emerald Street Boys

The two songs became a rap single on Benton's Telemusic label. Emerald Street Boys were now the reigning champions. They had basically stopped battling because they won every contest. Sweet J remembers how good it felt. "Nobody could beat us when we were at our peak," he says. The three rappers were head and shoulders above the rest.

They had their own record out on the shelves, and it was a remarkable hip hop achievement that no other local rap group had yet accomplished. "Christmas Rap" was no novelty tune, and the city noticed. Thanks to the music of Teleclere and the creative raps by the three young men, Emerald Street Boys were on the cutting edge of the new rap explosion. The influence of "Christmas Rap" immediately began to radiate throughout Seattle.

In 1984, SNECO kept Emerald Street Boys in the spotlight with their new production called *Showbizz*. In March that year, Empire Plaza hosted a showing of *Showbizz*. There was also a fall showing of *It's Entertainment Live* at Sidney's Restaurant and Cabaret.

FRESH TRACKS PROMOS

Since recording rap was still fairly new in 1983 and 1984, one of the few people aside from Benton to be ahead of the game was DJ Nasty-Nes. Nes had recorded promos for his *Fresh Tracks* show before, but one day, he got the idea to feature Seattle rappers in his promos. The station had already branded itself with round, bright yellow promotional stickers that read "KFOX 1250" and featured a clip art image of a fox.

KFOX promotional sticker. *Photograph by author.*

First, Nes turned to Emerald Street Boys, a group he was already familiar with due to the fact that he had DJed for some of their live shows. Emerald Street Boys recorded three intros for the *Fresh Tracks* show. Sweet J remembers recording the promos for *Fresh Tracks*. They would tape their raps at Nasty-Nes's Capitol Hill apartment or at the station itself.

The longest of the promos used Whodini's "Five Minutes of Funk" instrumental. The track featured a clever interpolation of the lyrics and tune for "When Doves Cry," by Prince. This first promo ran about three and a half minutes, as long as a full song.

Excerpt:

Nasty, Nasty mixing man
Make us a mix as fast as you can
Roll 'em, roll 'em, roll 'em good
On the turntable like you know you should

Dig if you will a DJ, with three MCs that turn out the mic
The beat of the music is louder, cut it faster, cut it fast tonight
The beat of your hands are amazing, how you handle 45s and 33s
The other DJs you will conquer, bring them down, down to their knees

Sugar Bear the name sounds so sweet
It echoes in your mind, makes your heartbeat
I'm the greatest and the latest MC on the block
To all the other rappers grab a piece of the rock
Because I really think you need it, cause I've never been defeated
I'll take your rhymes and spit them out and then I'll make you eat it

© 1983 Emerald Street Boys

The second intro was about two minutes long and included the *Addams Family* melody in one part of the rap. The group also stuck to business, shouting out the name of the station a few times and reminding the listeners the frequency was 1250 AM. Nes showed off his scratching chops in the background, as the group encouraged him to "Cut it up!"

Excerpt:

It's nine o'clock, it's time to rock, leave your radio on KFOX
The DJ gets fresh, he cuts the best, he goes by the name Nasty-Nes

Seattle listen up, yes it's just your luck
Nes is on the cut, KFOX Fresh Tracks
1250 on your dial, you're gonna keep your smile
We're gonna jam a while, back to back
Number one through the land KFOX is in command
They have a master plan

This is Sugar Bear, girls let me hear
Fresh Tracks *is on,* Fresh Tracks *is on*
This is Captain Crunch come join the fun
Fresh Tracks *is on,* Fresh Tracks *is on*
This is Sweet J, let me hear you say
Fresh Tracks *is on,* Fresh Tracks *is on*

We know you like the hits and the mix
And for your pleasure Nasty-Nes is gonna cut it up quick

When people come to see him, he has the cuts to greet them
His records are in a museum, they call him Nasty-Nes

© 1983 Emerald Street Boys

The last of the three promos was the shortest, at only one minute long. One verse was sung to the melody of the *Gilligan's Island* theme song. By using short popular melodies from TV or movies, MCs like Emerald Street Boys and others presented a cultural kaleidoscope for early '80s rap listeners.

Excerpt:

Who makes you rock from the tip of the top
Fresh Tracks *is on at nine o'clock*
Nasty-Nes play my favorite song
Yes I wanna hear it, hear it all night long

So sit right back and you'll hear the jams of DJ Nasty-Nes
And once the show is over you'll know he cuts it fresh

So slow down the pace and let's rock the bass
And let Nasty-Nes rock the whole human race
Just cut, cut the record and scratch, scratch the beat
Make us feel it over here down on Emerald Street

© 1983 Emerald Street Boys

These *Fresh Tracks* intros were some of the few raps ever recorded by Emerald Street Boys. Their "Christmas Rap" single was their only official release, and the group didn't put out a follow-up single until 2012.

The following year, in 1984, DJ Nasty-Nes made an intro with Jazzy D from the Silver Chain Gang. This one was produced by none other than Sir Mix-A-Lot. Jazzy D continued to pursue a solo career after Silver Chain Gang broke up. Jazzy D's verses on the promo were particularly rhythmic and symmetrical.

Excerpt:

The boy is fresh I must confess
And so will you because he cuts the best
In the Northwest, on the West Coast
I'm not trying to brag, I don't need to boast
But if you're missing just relax
Cause I've got 1250 KFOX Fresh Tracks

Nes is on time with the audio mixer
Scratch dominator and DJ fixer
On the beat box, two turntables
Rapping on records, a million labels
Can't be stopped cause he's at the top
Other DJs just beat rock
Plenty of power, always devour
Party nonstop for a serious hour
Striking up a storm, a sight to see
Fully dominating, unmistakably

© 1984 Jazzy D

Jazzy D effectively used pauses and short phrases in this promo. He was a very disciplined MC, and many producers, including Sir Mix-A-Lot, were interested in working with Jazzy D.

KNHC

DJ Nasty-Nes may have been dominating the rap radio game in Seattle, but there were other frequencies where the new musical genre peeked out. In addition to writing the "Sub Pop" column at *The Rocket*, Bruce Pavitt ran a radio show on KCMU, the University of Washington's campus radio station. Jonathan Poneman, the cofounder of Sub Pop Records, hosted a show there as well. They both might have sprinkled some rap into their shows from time to time. There was also a rap show at KRAB. But there was only one station where a true grassroots community was allowed to flourish.

A teacher named Larry Adams at Nathan Hale High School started a student-run FM radio station at the school in 1971. The call letters were KNHC, and the station played standard popular music mixed with news and public service announcements. Gregg Neilson came on board to become the general manager of the station. Adams and Neilson developed a program that allowed students to gain real-life radio experience and job training while still in high school.

Frank Higginbotham attended Sharples Junior High School and then Nathan Hale. Growing up, he was always interested in radio, and he listened to Gary Lockwood's show on KJR or *Murdock in the Morning* on KING. These hosts played a general top 40 format. By Higginbotham's junior year at Nathan Hale, he was the music director for KNHC. He graduated in 1981 and remained at the station for another year after that.

In his time on the air, Higginbotham remembers playing many of the early top hip hop songs of the day, including "Rapper's Delight," "The Breaks," "Double Dutch Bus" and "Egypt, Egypt." He would play a rap song, and then the phone would ring and the callers would ask, "Can you play that song again?" They wanted to hear the same songs over and over.

A 1981 *Seattle Sun* article by Ray Gastil described the state of the airwaves in Seattle in the early '80s. "You have to make an effort to hear rap on Seattle radio," Gastil pointed out. He then explained, "KNHC plays rhythm and blues with rap interspersed from 8 a.m. to 8 p.m. on weekends." Other stations, including KRAB and KFOX, are mentioned as well.

By 1981, KNHC had leaned pretty far into the hard rock format, according to Higginbotham. Soon, another Seattle rock station was upset that KNHC was infringing on their rock audience. As the music director, Higginbotham was tasked in early 1982 with switching the format of KNHC to something less rock-oriented.

One of the biggest changes was the addition of more Black artists on the playlist. Higginbotham remembers that it wasn't very complicated; he just wanted to try to bring to KNHC some of the great music he would hear in clubs around town. As music director, he was able to facilitate the arrival of more music from the Black community, including R&B and even a little rap.

One student DJ at the time, Wendi Dunlap, remembers the switch very well. According to Dunlap, "The station's entire non-R&B catalog had been removed and put in some cabinets in the music department." She continues, "We were told they were all going to the landfill, and I thought that was a tragedy." Dunlap jokes that she was able to "rescue" a few of the rock LPs thanks to her large backpack.

The switch to R&B was not without its bumps. During the 1982 New Year's Eve broadcast, Dunlap distinctly remembers a student playing the song "D.M.S.R." (Dance, Music, Sex, Romance), by Prince, and one of the teachers ran in and demanded that they take the record off immediately.

For some inappropriate songs, the censorship went even further. According to Dunlap, the teachers would vandalize the actual LP: "This could mean scratching the hell out of that track to make it unplayable, or painting it over with Liquid Paper."

After the rock-and-roll purge, the station needed more R&B music for the format shift, so Higginbotham would go to the record pools to get popular new releases. This led to meeting sales reps from MCA records and eventually receiving a job offer to work for MCA. Higginbotham took the job, which left him very little time for KNHC. Shortly after he left the station, the "C-89" nickname was born. Starting around 1983, C-89 quickly became the popular shorthand name for the station.

Another young DJ at KNHC in the '80s was Shamseddin "Shomps" Williams. Shomps attended Rainier Beach High School, and even though he wasn't a student at Nathan Hale, he was encouraged to join the radio program. "There weren't that many opportunities for young Black men like myself," remembers Shomps. According to Higginbotham, both Larry Adams and Gregg Neilson made a conscious effort to recruit students from other schools throughout the city.

When he first arrived at KNHC, Shomps was happy to see another Black student named John Blanks in the program. Blanks was already an on-air personality who went by the nickname of "Jam Man." According to Shomps, Jam Man was a true trailblazer in the mostly white radio program.

Shomps sometimes brought his own albums to play on the air. During 1982 and 1983, Jam Man and Shomps would both host programs on Saturdays; Jam Man would do the earlier shift and Shomps would do the later one. Shomps remembers that "Kickin Kevin" Jones sometimes dropped by the station, and he showed Shomps how to do little DJ turntable tricks that he could add to his repertoire. He also recalls that Tony Benton from Teleclere would hang out and do work at the station from time to time.

Keith "Sergio Lacour" Samuels is the younger brother of LaSalle "Duke of Earl" Samuels from Silver Chain Gang. Samuels recounts that one of his first rap-based experiences occurred while he was a high school student in Tulsa, Oklahoma. A local radio station had a call-in portion of the show in which listeners could call and shout out their names and where they were

(*Clockwise from the top*) Frank Barrow, Joseph "Run" Simmons, Daryl "DMC" McDaniels and Keith "Sergio Lacour" Samuels. *Photograph courtesy of Keith Samuels.*

from. Usually, it was something like, "I'm so and so, and I go to such and such high school."

Samuels and his friends were listening, so they called in. When it was their turn to say their names, they started rapping instead, and the rap went out live over the airwaves. In a way, it was similar to Kickin Kevin Jones's experience at Wide World of Music a few years prior. The station host was so impressed that he invited Samuels to come visit the studio. Samuels was amazed at all the knobs and dials he saw there. He spent as much time as possible at the station to learn the ins and outs of broadcasting.

Then for his senior year of high school, Samuels moved from Tulsa to Seattle and began attending Nathan Hale High School. According to Samuels, one of the first people he met was Sir Wes from Silver Chain Gang, who was very friendly to him. This helped him feel more at home in Seattle. Samuels quickly gravitated toward the KNHC radio program and was excited to be a part of the station. He clearly remembers memorizing the station motto to repeat on the air: "C-89, Dance Music Radio."

As a disc jockey, Samuels was mostly geared toward broadcasting, but he still DJed for fun at house parties and get-togethers whenever he could. Samuels knew lots of DJ tricks and chose the stage name "DJ Sergio Lacour."

He has memories of often riding the route no. 7 or no. 48 Metro bus to parties while carrying a crate full of records.

Lacour later worked at Seattle station KRIZ and was lucky enough to be in the studio when Run DMC visited from New York. Local broadcasting veteran Frank Barrow was there that day as well, and Lacour still has a very special photograph of himself and Barrow with rap music legends Joseph "Run" Simmons and Daryl "DMC" McDaniels.

SOUNDS OF SEATTLE

Sir Lover the MC was still working at Dirt Cheap Records. One day, Sir Lover remembers being in the arcade above the shop, looking down to the street and seeing a huge brawl break out. There had been some bullies who harassed the neighborhood kids, and someone had decided to finally put a stop to it. The melee was unlike anything Sir Lover had ever seen. The bullies lost that day, and order was restored around the Twenty-Third Avenue and Union Street block.

The next day, word traveled through the grapevine that some of the guys who had won the fight were from Syracuse, New York. Sir Lover the MC got a call from his friend Michael Turner, who said that the New York dudes were starting a rap crew called Sounds of Seattle (SOS) and that they were going to have tryouts for new rappers. Sir Lover really wanted to get in, so he went and auditioned. SOS liked what they heard and inducted him into the SOS crew. Sir Lover was finally a member of a real rap group.

Allen "DJ Grand Electric Captain Luv" Lynch from Syracuse, New York, was the frontman of SOS, and he was an early style icon in the Seattle rap world. Captain Luv was tall with green eyes, and he would always be sporting the finest Kangol or Adidas gear. He would often walk around with a giant pair of headphones on his head, just as a fashion accessory. "Captain Luv was New York personified," as Frostmaster Chill remembers.

Lou "DJ Skego" Morgan was Captain Luv's uncle, and he was also important to the success of SOS. When he mixed records, DJ Skego was the master of the blend, and he owned an enormous mobile sound system that he brought everywhere. Having a good inventory in the crate was crucial, because at the time, most rappers simply rapped over instrumentals. Captain Luv and DJ Skego had all the best records, and somehow, they could get copies of instrumentals that nobody else had in Seattle. This made SOS formidable to battle, because they had the freshest background beats.

Michael "DJ EZ Shock" Turner was a young teenager whose main love was basketball. He grew up in a home that always had a record player, and his parents kept albums, like those from Earth Wind & Fire, Lakeside and Gap Band, on the shelf. "Rapper's Delight" hadn't really captured his imagination, but then in 1981, Tom Tom Club's "Genius of Love" came out, and his ear was hooked on the jolty, melodic production. The single came with an instrumental, and Turner was very excited. He tried to rap over the beat and even teamed up with a neighborhood friend named Keith Beaver. They called themselves the 20th Street Boys.

A jacket worn by Allen "Captain Luv" Lynch. *Jacket courtesy of David Blanchard, photograph by author.*

Michael "DJ EZ Shock" Turner. *Photograph courtesy of Michael Turner.*

Turner had a hoop outside his house to practice in his spare time. One day during Turner's freshman year at Ballard High School, a fresh dressed b-boy came up and asked, "Can I ball with you guys?" After the game, they were sitting around, and the dude finally told them his name: Grand Electric Captain Luv.

Captain Luv later brought Turner to a cousin's house, and Turner saw there was a pair of turntables set up in a closet, just like a club booth. He decided to become a DJ for real, and his first name was "DJ EZ EZ," (pronounced "easy ease"). Captain Luv had a Technics 1500 and a 1600, and they used those for a while. Turner recalls that their first mixer was a Realistic, and then they got a slightly better Numark. Turner learned to mix from Captain Luv, who was brilliant at scratching. In fact, Captain Luv would bring back one-sided records from New York that were easier to manipulate because there were no grooves on the opposite side to drag against whatever he was using as a slipmat.

Turner had a brother, Leonard "Luv Jones," and a sister, Felicia, who were both very intimidating and served as security for the events and parties. If a guy was acting out, Luv Jones would handle it. But if a woman got wild, Felicia would be the one to solve the problem.

The first SOS party where Turner played records was up in the Northgate area of Seattle. This was his first real gig, and he was a little scared. Someone told him, "Just don't let there be any dead space." He started his set with "It's Like That," by Run DMC, and things were going well, but then the record ended more suddenly than Turner thought, and there was a short, awkward silence. He never forgot that moment and vowed to always have his next song cued up in time.

Now SOS was a full crew that included Captain Luv, DJ Skego, Sir Lover the MC and Turner. Around this time, at the advice of Captain Luv, Turner changed his name from DJ EZ EZ to "DJ EZ Shock."

There was also a Junior SOS crew of younger rappers that included more than a dozen young, aspiring MCs. One of the best places where SOS performed was a house at Twentieth Avenue and Pine Street. According to Sir Lover the MC, this house was the McDaniels' residence, and there were lots of house parties there every Friday and Saturday for a while. They would set up the mic and turntables in one of the bedrooms and rock the party from there.

Captain Luv remembers those Twentieth Avenue and Pine Street parties very well. "We could make $500 on a Friday night, and then make $700 on Saturday," he says. They had to charge only $1 a head to get in, and the people came in large numbers.

He also recalls a flawlessly executed party at the famous Washington Hall. Renting Washington Hall could be accomplished for about $100. Captain Luv asked his mom to borrow $150 and threw a party at Washington Hall. He brought in $700, paid back his mom and still had a nice profit. They also hosted events at Campfire House and another popular Seattle venue called the Mountaineers Club.

There was a crew of ten or twelve young women associated with SOS, and they were called The Backbreakers. Captain Luv developed the perfect strategy to feature them dancing at parties where SOS performed. Just as festivities got started around 9:00 p.m., the Backbreakers were already there having a good time. Any guys who looked inside would see the girls dancing and happily pay the money at the door to get in. The Backbreakers had T-shirts and jackets with their names and "SOS Backbreakers" on them.

One of the Backbreakers was named "All Butter," and she was the loudest of them according to Frostmaster Chill. She would act as a distraction in any battle, yelling and cussing at the opponents to rattle them. Captain Luv remembers the Backbreakers fondly. "Sticky Wicky," "Bussit Lisa" and "Lovin' Gemini" are some names he summons up from his memory.

Captain Luv recalls that Q Boys were the main competition. He gives them credit for throwing live parties in the early '80s. But Captain Luv claims that the SOS parties had better DJs.

Later, Baron Von Scratch and Mix-A-Lot battled SOS in the South End. Mix and Baron set up five turntables on their side, plus a foot pedal. Captain Luv's mixing and scratching were pretty good, but Baron Von Scratch was clearly the tightest DJ in the battle. But then All Butter jumped up and yelled foul. Mix-A-Lot was using tapes, not live mixing, she accused. Mix often included recorded audio with his live performances and made no secret of it, but in this battle, it was called a foul. Chaos ensued, and the battle was called a draw due to not officially being complete.

Captain Luv once set up his turntables at Garfield High School and challenged all comers to a DJ battle. Frostmaster Chill decided to accept the challenge and stepped up to the decks. Unfortunately, Captain Luv had his layout customized and had a different brand of turntable, which was awkward for Frostmaster. Frostmaster wasn't used to mixing on Captain Luv's turntables, and he remembers that his mix didn't go as well as he wanted. Captain Luv was judged to be the winner by the crowd. That day, Frostmaster decided he was going to get his own professional turntables.

"7 RAINIER"

Anthony "Sir Mix-A-Lot" Ray had become a bit of a known quantity in the music world now that he was settled in Rainier Beach. He had started referring to himself as the "Computerized DJ." Mix-A-Lot often hung out with Jerome "Baron Von Scratch" Gibson since they both lived on South Henderson Street.

Meanwhile, Sir Mix-A-Lot had already fallen in love with DJing and gotten his first set of turntables. He embraced his role DJing for Jam Delight, and hearing Big Boss Cross rap left a very strong impression. According to Mix-A-Lot, Big Boss Cross was different than other rappers. Mix explains, "Most rappers wanted to battle but Cross just wanted to brag about how

Metro bus route no. 7. *Photograph courtesy of the Puget Sound Regional Archives.*

cool he was." One of Cross's lines that Mix remembers is "I know you love my Jheri curl."

Until this point, Mix-A-Lot hadn't really considered himself a rapper, so he was curious to try it. As an experiment, he recorded raps in his bedroom, but there was an echo that ruined the sound. So, he put a blanket over his head and tried it that way. However, the blanket would rub against the mic, which made a different kind of background noise. So, as Mix-A-Lot recalls, he taped a ruler to the back of a mic stand to keep the blanket and microphone from touching.

Sir Mix-A-Lot was a big fan of Egyptian Lover, a popular beat programmer and DJ in Los Angeles. Egyptian Lover had dominated the dancefloors of 1983 with Uncle Jams Army's "Dial a Freak" and then his own solo cut "Egypt, Egypt" the following year. These fast and futuristic West Coast beats were computerized, inspiring Mix-A-Lot to teach himself the art of electronic drum sequencing.

German electronic group Kraftwerk was also a big influence for Mix-A-Lot. As soon as he saw the four of them onstage with their hand-built synthesizers, Mix knew he wanted to make his own version. Kraftwerk's use of computers in their music also rubbed off on Mix, and he incorporated his own Commodore 64 into the recording process. The robotic-sounding drum machines of pop groups like Devo definitely played a role as well.

Rainier Avenue is a major arterial road running through south Seattle. Mix-A-Lot made a track called "7 Rainier" about the no. 7 Metro bus line that ran up and down Rainier Avenue. The beat was inspired by *The Man-Machine*, by Kraftwerk, and Baron Von Scratch recalls helping Mix replay the melody on a keyboard. Then they put together the beat.

The song "7 Rainier" was a huge local hit because so many South End residents relied on that exact bus to get from neighborhood to neighborhood. Sir Mix-A-Lot was actually rapping about things that young people experienced in their daily Seattle routines, which drove home the connection to the song.

In fact, Mix-A-Lot was ridiculously prolific at this Rainier Beach apartment, creating dozens of unique songs in his bedroom studio with barely any gear. Baron Von Scratch remembers an early song by Mix-A-Lot called "Why Do the Rappers Lie?"

Many of his tracks were parodies of popular songs like "Erotic City," by Prince, or "Cruisin," by Smokey Robinson, in a style similar to Weird Al Yankovic. Mix made a song called "High School Ducks" that was modeled after "Buffalo Gals," by Malcolm McLaren. "Roxanne Gets Cut" was a riff on "Roxanne Roxanne" by popular New York group UTFO.

Speaking of UTFO, another early Sir Mix-A-Lot rap, "Mixmaster Ice Can't Hang," was a dis track targeted at the group's DJ. At the end of the track, Mix-A-Lot gives Mixmaster Ice an imaginary haircut, with little scissor snip sounds made by the record scratch. When asked if the song ever reached Mixmaster Ice at the time, Mix-A-Lot laughs. "Thank God it didn't; he would have kicked my ass."

By 1984, each of these songs had built up a huge local market of Mix-A-Lot fans. The airtime also cemented the relationship between Mix-A-Lot the musician and DJ Nasty-Nes the radio host. More original song titles included "My Coupe," "British Rap," "Theme Song," "Computer Freak" and "High Class." Each of these songs was funky and different, and DJ Nasty-Nes played them on *Fresh Tracks* to delighted listeners. On the song "Deadbeat," the lyrics directly reference "7 Rainier": "Where's your beatbox Mix-A-Lot Ray? Where's 7 Rainier?" asks the high-pitched, robotic voice.

The Smurf/Chipmunk voice sound was very popular in this era. Mix-A-Lot had figured out how to do many variations of this using electronics and other audio tools. Baron Von Scratch remembers asking Mix-A-Lot to explain the technique and then trading gear with Mix to get his own Smurf voice on his mixtapes. Neither of them had any idea how consequential that helium-inspired voice would become.

"SUPERSONIC RAP"

Charles "C.T." Thompson. *Photograph courtesy of Charles Thompson.*

Charles "C.T." Thompson was a musician in Seattle, and in 1980, he decided to start his own record label. C.T. had several reasons to start the label. He was determined to be a success, and he didn't want another company taking all the profits. If he was independent, he would have more control. Another big reason to own his own label was the fact that he would never have to face rejections from submitting to other companies.

First, he had to choose a name for his business, and he decided on Kalieba Records, which incorporated letters from some of his family members' names. The "ka" came from one name, the "li" from another and so on. He hired a music lawyer to create the paperwork, and soon, he had his own business. His group was called C.T. and the Record Band.

The first single on Kalieba Records, "Can't Live Without You," was actually produced by David "Little Ray Rapper" Perry. The label's second release was a track called "On My Way to Mississippi." These songs were released on seven-inch, 45 RPM records.

Meanwhile, the Seattle Supersonics basketball team won the national NBA title in 1979, and the city celebrated the victory for several years. In

1983, C.T. got a job working at Lateef's. He remembers that one day, he was talking with Lester Green about this new genre called rap. Lester pointed out to C.T. that nobody had done a rap about the Sonics yet. C.T. was an observer of rap music from the sidelines, but he felt it was definitely more than just a fad. He suspected it would be around for a long time.

C.T. and Lester realized that writing a rap about the Sonics could be a good idea, so C.T. wrote it. In 1983, he recorded the song at Northwest Studio, which was located in north Seattle near Eighty-Fifth Street and Greenwood Avenue. In 1984, the song was released as a seven-inch single on C.T.'s Kalieba Records. According to C.T., he made five hundred copies of the record.

Excerpt:

I say come on fans and clap your hands
And participate with the Record Band
Say let's go Sonics and cheer them on
To be the best in the land
Well, they've been world champs once before
They're gonna be world champs a few times more
So let's stay in their corner at all times
Cause this is our team and they're one of a kind

There's Gus Williams, the play making wizard
He knows how to shoot that ball
And in every game you'll always feel
That he's going to give his all
Jack Sikma, Jack Sikma
Aw you shoot so strange
But when in range the points will change
"Mr. Rebound" I hope you remain
Now "Downtown" Freddy Brown
He seems to never let you down
By making shots you can't believe
And giving lots of spirit to the team

Let's go Sonics all the way
And be the champs of the NBA

© 1983 C.T. Thompson

"Supersonic Rap." © *1983 Kalieba Records, scan by author.*

According to Roberta Penn, writing in *The Rocket*, the song "Supersonic Rap" was "written for but not a hit with the Sonics basketball team." C.T. explains that it wasn't quite that simple. He remembers that when he contacted the team's management and gave them a copy of the record, the response was positive. "They actually played it at about twenty or thirty home games," recalls C.T.

The Seattle Supersonics organization liked the song enough to discuss licensing or buying it from C.T. and the Record Band. Unfortunately, the details proved to be quite extensive. C.T.'s lawyer made a contract to give to the Sonics, but eventually, the team rejected C.T.'s offer. When asked if he did any other rap songs at the time, C.T. replies, "No, ['Supersonic Rap'] was it."

However, C.T. does remember a rap he wrote many years later called "Prime Time." This track, which he cocreated with Seattle musician Michael Powers, referenced the 2010 New Orleans Saints, who won the Superbowl. According to Thompson, "Prime Time" is not really about football; it's more about staying true to your goals and accomplishing your dreams.

1984

KINGS OF CUTS

At some point, Sounds of Seattle (Captain Luv, Skego, DJ EZ Shock and Sir Lover the MC) were pressured to stop using the SOS name. A street gang also called SOS raised objections to Sounds of Seattle using the same letters. There was beef for a while, and finally, the gang convinced Captain Luv's rap crew to stop using SOS.

Sounds of Seattle then changed their name to Kings of Cuts, or KOC for short. Occasionally, the name variation "Kings of Cutting" was also used. KOC added an MC named "Master T" to their group. Master T was small and dapper; they sometimes called him "Lil Pimpy." Both Captain Luv and EZ Shock had shiny custom belt buckles with their names on them.

David "Daddy D" Blanchard attended Washington Middle School and then Roosevelt High School, and he joined SOS/KOC just before the name change. The new posse felt like more than just a hip hop crew; it had elements of a gang. According to Daddy D, they would battle other crews with raps, but there were times that the rap battles would become fistfights. What made Daddy D stand out wasn't just his young age; he was also the only white rapper in a scene that was exclusively made up of Black artists. He remembers being referred to as the "Ivory Kid" by other rappers.

New York rapper Melle Mel was Daddy D's idol, thanks to his conscious, hard-hitting tracks like "The Message." Daddy D was drawn to political and social awareness, and he began to pepper his raps with references to Ronald Reagan and other political figures.

As Daddy D recalls, Captain Luv really welcomed him into the group and took him under his wing as a kind of student. One early KOC party routine started with Captain Luv saying, "Attention, attention, all hands on deck. Daddy D is on the mic, and he demands respect." Then Daddy D would repeat the whole line, finishing with, "I demand respect," and the crowds would go wild.

David "Daddy D" Blanchard.
Photograph courtesy of David Blanchard.

Daddy D's mother remembers those days when Captain Luv would be at her house a lot. For some reason, Captain Luv would always be on the phone, she says. But then she got a phone bill with hundreds of dollars' worth of calls to New York. She laughs about it now, but at the time, she was very upset and demanded that he not use their phone for free. That put a stop to Captain Luv's long-distance-call hustle.

Meanwhile, Frostmaster Chill and Mellow Mike hadn't worked together since the days of Cosmic Crew, but circumstances brought them back in contact. Frostmaster teamed up with Mellow Mike again, just like in the old days, and the two regained status as battlers. Daddy D remembers that the KOC crew had a major showdown with Frostmaster Chill and Mellow Mike.

The way Daddy D remembers it, the battle was epic, like the Greeks versus the Trojans. KOC had more members, with three rappers and two DJs, but during the battle, it became clear that Frostmaster was really crushing it on the wheels against Captain Luv and EZ Shock. The rhymers Daddy D, Sir Lover and Master T tried their rapping best against Mellow Mike. Master T had long hair at the time, and he wore a kitchen-style hairnet to the battle for extra flair.

Because the DJ beatdown was going so badly for KOC, Mellow Mike salted the wound by directing one of his raps at EZ Shock, really trying to insult him. EZ Shock didn't think it was fair for Mellow Mike to insult the DJ. It was supposed to be a rapper-versus-rapper battle. EZ Shock tried to fight with Mellow Mike, and the chaos ended the battle.

Another battle was between KOC and a team of Deputy Rhyme and a rapper named "MC Poncho." This one got really heated, with personal jabs added to the raps. According to Sir Lover the MC, he said some derogatory raps about MC Poncho's mother, and Poncho wasn't happy. Poncho approached Sir Lover and punched him before Sir Lover could even finish his verse.

According to Sir Lover, KOC faced off against Mix-A-Lot at Rainier Vista. At one point, EZ Shock yelled out that Mix-A-Lot was cheating because he was using recorded music on a four-track. Although Mix had faced this accusation before, tensions started to rise. Captain Luv told Sir Lover the MC to go out to the car, remembering there was an old turntable that wasn't too valuable in the trunk.

Sir Lover the MC carried the turntable from the car into the middle of the gym where the battle was taking place, and he lifted it dramatically over his head until everyone was looking at him. Then he smashed it on the floor angrily to protest. The turntable loudly broke into pieces, stunning the crowd. Sir Lover yelled, "F— the South End!" as loudly as he could, and instantly, people jumped up and started to fight. It was a brawl, and Sir Lover remembers it was difficult to safely get through the melee to escape. Sir Lover admits that he was a part of the rivalry between the Central District and the South End. In fact, he says, "We're the reason Southcenter [shopping mall] has security."

At one point, Afrika Bambaataa came to Seattle to perform and did a set at a local club. Captain Luv had been involved with setting up the show, and KOC were the opening act. Daddy D rapped, and EZ Shock scratched on the wheels of steel. The breakers loved it, and the energy in the room was electric. According to EZ Shock, he saw DJ Nasty-Nes from KFOX walking across the room. Everyone knew Nasty-Nes; he was a city celebrity as the DJ for *Fresh Tracks*. Nes stood there, watching the turntables and bobbing his head. EZ Shock was doing all the tricks that Captain Luv had taught him, plus some of his own tricks.

During one trick, Nasty-Nes leaned in, pointed to the wheels and asked, "Can you show me how to do that?" This rubbed EZ Shock the wrong way. Nes was just trying to be friendly, but EZ Shock was pissed. According to EZ, he was mad because, even though KOC had sent songs to Nes, they never heard them played on the air on KFOX. "I've been sending you tapes for over a year, and you ignored us," EZ Shock blurted out. Nasty-Nes just stood there confused. Then EZ Shock turned away, saying, "Talk to Daddy D." And he left the stage.

EZ Shock was friendly with Sir Mix-A-Lot, and they talked from time to time. But Mix-A-Lot had some beef with Captain Luv, so there was never a lot of connection between the two camps. In the KOC era, EZ Shock remembers a woman rapper named Lisa who was thuggish and could crush all her adversaries. Another lady MC who was down with the crew was named Candy.

KOC was always battling. Baron Von Scratch remembers battling the KOC crew in 1984. Baron and Mix-A-Lot were a team against KOC. Mix-A-Lot had the drum machines going, but KOC complained about that. So, Baron and Mix turned off the beat machine and just went off the turntables. Baron cut up the Captain Rock song "Cosmic Blast" and used a delay pedal to make the record sound supernatural. The crowd exploded, and the winners of the battle were Baron and Mix-A-Lot.

Sometimes, these battles or performances would spontaneously occur in parking lots right along South Henderson Street, the street where Baron, Mix-A-Lot and Stephen "Kid Sensation" Spence all lived. Baron recalls that there was a Seafirst bank across the street from his house that had an outdoor electrical outlet from which he could easily get power. Once the music was playing, a crowd would gather. Baron also became an expert in figuring out how to break into the bases of streetlights to power his music that way.

Eventually, KOC began to fall apart. Captain Luv moved out of town to Nevada, which left the group without their flashiest star. DJ EZ Shock started to get distracted with the street life, which affected his musical career. Daddy D was still rapping, and he went solo for a while. Sir Lover actually got kicked out of his house and moved into Frostmaster Chill's house at Nineteenth Avenue and Union Street.

"I PITY THE MAN"

Seattle breakdancing veteran Carlos Barrientes grew up and attended junior high in Seattle, and then around 1980, he went to high school in Texas. But during high school, he skipped class a lot, and his dad told him he either needed take school seriously or drop out and get a job. So, Barrientes dropped out of school to work full time. Word about a b-boy crew called Emerald City Breakers that was way up in Seattle traveled to Texas. He wasn't really into rapping or tagging, but he loved the breakdancing culture that was sparking across the world.

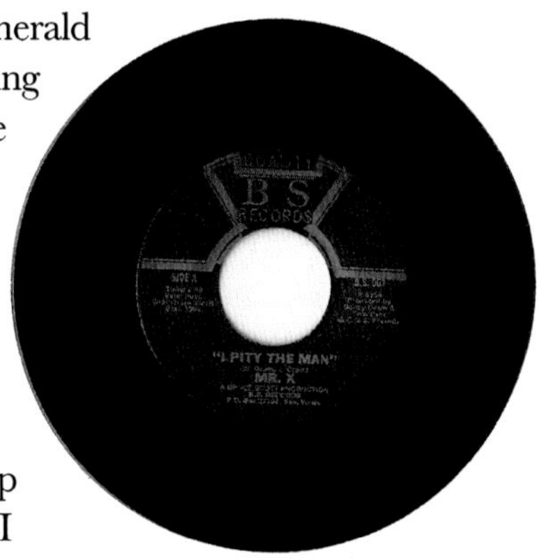

"I Pity the Man." © *1984 BS Records, scan by author.*

Barrientes decided he wanted to join the Emerald City Breakers group and ended up moving back to Seattle in 1982. But not long after he returned, the Emerald City Breakers split up, and in the aftermath, Barrientes helped found a new crew. Barrientes recalls, "1983 is when Jay Bateman, Rey Martinez [formerly Rey Bell] and I left ECB and formed Seattle City Breakers."

An interesting parody record popped up around Seattle in 1984. The song's title, "I Pity the Man," was nearly identical to the catchphrase "I pity the fool," made popular by Mr. T's television character on *The A-Team*. The performer on the Seattle record went by the name "Mr. X" and remained anonymous.

Bobby and Jack Oram are credited with writing the lyrics. "I Pity the Man" was released on BS Records, a label founded by Bruce Scott. Imitating Mr. T, Seattle's Mr. X used a gruff voice for his parody rap. Mr. T had actually put out his own rap record, titled *Mr. T's Commandments*, that same year.

One day, the Seattle City Breakers' manager Jim Clark called Barrientes and told him about tryouts for a music video. Seattle City Breakers gave it their best at the audition, and they were selected to appear in "I Pity the Man." The video was shot at the Blue Moon Tavern near the University of Washington and was directed by local filmmaker Karl Krogstad. It featured breakdancers from various Seattle b-boy crews to match the hip hop vibe of the song. Rey Martinez was the youngest b-boy in the Seattle City Breakers crew, and as the star of the shoot, he got most of the camera time.

Similar to "I'm Little Ray Rapper," "I Pity the Man" used humor and novelty in a rap context. This showed that here in Seattle and across America, rap music was slowly becoming part of the common musical language. It was creeping into mainstream culture one song at a time.

Excerpt:

I pity the man who takes what I got
I pity that man if he can't take a shot
I pity the chump who thinks he's more manly
I'll hit him so hard it'll bruise his whole dang family

I pity the man who moves in on my action
I pity that man, I'll put him in traction
I pity the sucker who gives no respect
I'll knock him clear into payday, then I'll cancel his check

© *1984 Mr. X*

The B-side of "I Pity the Man" was the same musical bed, but the rap lyrics were gone. Instead, Mr. X just occasionally riffed like a comedy routine, staying in the character. He started on a meta note. "You're still here?" he asked, pretending to be surprised that the listener flipped over the record. Backup singers repeated over and over "he's bad," and they also talked about Mr. X's physical characteristics, including the fact that his hair was shaved into an "X" on the top of his head.

DANNY DEE ROCK

Danny "Dee Rock" Clavesilla was always a fan of music. One of his hobbies as a kid was collecting soul and R&B records. His parents bought him children's records, but he was more interested in their collection than the music made for kids. He remembers getting a copy of "Rapture," by Blondie, and being entranced with the sound. Of course, "Rapper's Delight" was another early record he remembers collecting. Clavesilla would buy anything on Sugar Hill Records, with the notable candy-swirl sleeve to alert him.

Clavesilla got involved in hip hop very early on, thanks to his interest in BMX bike racing. Around 1981, he traveled to New York, and his experience was recorded by *Vibrant* magazine in 2019. "The [BMX] tour took young Danny all the way to the East Coast, with several days spent in New York City. In the neighborhood that Danny's group was staying, something unusual was happening," wrote the magazine. The story continued, "Each night, dozens of people would bring their radios down to the park, tuning them all to the same station to listen to DJ Red Alert."

The article went on to describe the birth of breakdancing, "There was something else happening as well—a new dance form was emerging. Kids jumping and kicking, pointing and spinning. Danny was fascinated by what he saw."

Danny "Dee Rock" Clavesilla. *Photograph courtesy of Danny Clavesilla.*

Clavesilla returned to Seattle, energized about music and also breaking. He formed a breakdance crew called Seattle Circuit Breakers. His mother managed the group, even landing a sponsorship from Adidas sportswear. When Mattel introduced a toy drum pad called Synsonics, Clavesilla immediately got one. But he soon needed to upgrade. Over the next several years, Clavesilla started acquiring better gear. Soon, he had picked a nickname, "Danny Dee Rock."

By the time he was a student at Ballard High School, Danny Dee Rock was also an aspiring hip hop producer who had a rudimentary bedroom studio. To get more equipment, the process was pretty simple. There were certain Ballard students known as "boosters," who were basically professional shoplifters. You could give the booster twenty bucks on Friday, and on Monday, he would come back with a new Polo sweater or a pair of Nikes. Danny Dee Rock quickly figured out that he could ask these guys if they knew how to get electronics.

On Friday, Danny Dee Rock would give someone forty or fifty bucks, and by Monday, he would have a new sampler or even a keyboard. His bedroom got more and more packed with gear, and he learned how to use it all. He started making drumbeats with no music, just like Run DMC had done on "Sucker MCs" and other early songs. Dee Rock would tape DJ Nasty-Nes on KFOX whenever his *Fresh Tracks* show was on.

Danny Dee Rock was very curious about the tools used to make hip hop. A music store called Kinelly Keys had some knowledgeable staff, and Dee Rock often traveled to the store to ask questions. "What's a drum machine?"

was one of the first. The staff carefully explained what different pieces of gear could do. When he heard a robotic voice on Roger and Zapp songs, he asked the Kinelly staff how it was done, and they explained that it was called a vocoder.

In 1983, Cornel "C.M.T." Thomas was a freshman at Ingraham High School who liked music and art. Interestingly, the 1983 Ingraham High School yearbook featured a huge photograph of a turntable on the cover. The year and title were written on the record label, and the image feels very hip hop inspired.

Danny Dee Rock and C.M.T. were introduced by Fever, a talented breaker in the Seattle b-boy scene. Soon, Dee Rock and C.M.T. were hanging out often. C.M.T. was very gifted with electronics and learned how to make beats along with Dee Rock. Together, they came up with the name Incredicrew for their production duo.

In a 2020 interview with PIG Records, Dee Rock remembered, "When we met, we just clicked and became best friends instantly." They would go to record stores and hit the nightclubs on weekends. Dee Rock recalled that C.M.T. was always sketching on paper, and his drawings were amazing.

"I had a [Roland] 808, and he came by the house and asked if he could use it," remembered Dee Rock. Dee Rock said he could, and then just minutes later, C.M.T. had already figured out how to make a beat. Dee Rock was amazed, because it was a complicated drum machine.

At least once a week, Incredicrew would go record shopping together at Musicland in downtown Seattle. There was a good chance that someone would have a boombox and some cardboard set up nearby, maybe at Westlake Center or in front of McDonalds. This meant that there would be b-boys to watch and usually some dope music to listen to.

Rappers began to call Incredicrew to ask them for beats. They acquired a four-track recorder and were able to mix rap demos for clients. Dee Rock and C.M.T. never even thought to charge money for the service. It was cool enough just to have your beat on someone's tape.

Sometime around 1985, Gary Jam from Jam Delight heard about Incredicrew and contacted them. They gave Gary Jam a beat for a track, and Jam wrote a rap called "Funky Fresh Beat of the Drum." Danny Dee Rock knew about a Seattle recording studio called Music Source, so he booked time there to get a good quality sound. "Funky Fresh Beat of the Drum" is a terrific achievement. Gary Jam had a flow that was catchy and fun; in this track, it almost resembled the cadence of Whodini on songs like "Echo Scratch."

Excerpt:

Without further ado, I introduce to you
Myself, Gary Jam making my debut
I should win an award as rap's best newcomer
Cause I'mma go off with this funky fresh drummer
I paid my dues and now here I am
This is my very first record and I know it's a jam
I'm from the old school but I was not a household name
So now it's time I break out and take my claim to fame

To be a part of hip hop, it's all non-stop
Fresh beats so hard now they're calling it pop
Raps are on the charts hitting number one
Gold records and tours have now been done
Cause it's a B-Boy's dream to have the self esteem
And recognition into the music mainstream
And now that it's arrived you can all get some
Of course I'm talking about the funky fresh beat of the drum

Cause as long as the funky beat is deffer than def
I'm gonna serve ya like a famous world renowned chef
I got a menu that could truly be the main appetizer
Just listen to the words of Gary Jam the mesmerizer
If you got enough room for the fresh dessert
I'm gonna bring the house down and cause a red alert
Because it's all about dancing till your feet get numb
But when you're dancing to the funky fresh beat of the drum

© *1985 Gary Jam*

Danny Dee Rock got his first DJ gig at a small club in Federal Way. He showed up confident in his DJing ability and started doing hip hop–style tricks during his set. But right away, people stopped dancing because Dee Rock was cutting and scratching too much. He quickly realized that keeping a dance floor moving required patience and strategy. This ability to read the room was a skill that he intended to learn.

SUMMER BREAK

In 1984, the City of Seattle held an event called "Summer Break." Steve Sneed of SNECO was the MC of the event. Emerald Street Boys were still the godfathers of the Seattle rap scene, and they were hired by the show's promoters to perform a rap at the beginning and end of the competition. The contest was one of the first big hip hop breakdancing events that was citywide.

The *Seattle Times* newspaper published a buzzy feature story on February 19 that year about the explosion of breakdancing culture. Breaking's popularity certainly contributed to KOMO Channel 4's decision to broadcast the Summer Break competition during primetime. The one-hour show aired on September 1, 1984, followed by *T.J. Hooker* and then two hours of *Love Boat*. Popular local news personality Steve Pool recorded some clips that explained the culture, and these lighthearted segments were interspersed between rounds of the dance competition.

It was a huge win for hip hop culture in Seattle, and the show raised awareness of the b-boy movement in the city. One of the dance groups competing was called High Performance, and they later evolved from breaking to rapping. Danny Dee Rock's group Seattle Circuit Breakers and Carlos Barrientes's crew the Seattle City Breakers both competed.

The Emerald Street Boys' rapping performance at Summer Break was flawless. The three of them were dressed in the latest fashions of rap music. Two movies that year, *Beat Street* and *Breakin'*, had helped define the hip hop look. Captain Crunch dressed in all black with dark glasses, while Sugar Bear looked sparkling in all white. Sweet J wore bright blue, and he rocked shorts instead of pants. They comfortably commanded the large stage with the synchronized dance moves that had taken them to the top.

Excerpt:

C'mon party people wave your hands in the air
For the Captain, Sweet J, and Sugar Bear
We're gonna have a party that you don't want to miss
We need your crowd participation and it goes like this

They say the other rappers can't do it like this
If they come against the Boys it's at their own risk
We have a show that always breaks no one can ever imitate

We're the cream of the crop, we're the icing on the cake
We're gonna take you to the top, while we break it on down
If you wanna party hearty then you gotta stick around
But it's just like the Boys to make you feel good
Because we rock it and don't stop it like you knew we would

© *1984 Emerald Street Boys*

All three recited some parts together and then broke the lyrics into several phrases that they took turns rapping. Then they led the crowd in a call-and-response chant: "Seattle rocks without a doubt. The Street Boys turn the party out." The crowd loved it and loudly cheered along. The KOMO Summer Break broadcast brought hip hop and rap from the heart of Seattle into living rooms all over the Pacific Northwest.

The director of Summer Break, Dave Schnuckel, remembers filming the preliminary rounds and then shooting the final competition at Seattle Center. He and his team were very proud of the finished video. "We even sent it to a film and TV festival in New York," he recalls. Even though his personal music tastes were not geared to rap, he had a positive experience at the event.

"COME AND GET SOME BOYS"

DJ Mike Joyce from Lateef's had continued making a name for himself, and he had landed some good DJ gigs around town, including a residency at Club Broadway. Joyce was still teamed up with "Kickin" Kevin Jones, who would operate the lights at the club while Joyce mixed.

Joyce would even let aspiring MCs improvise raps over his instrumentals. He would sometimes record cassette tapes of the live performances to listen to and critique later. On one memorable Club Broadway tape from this era, a young rapper named "L Starr Lamar" gets loose on a long freestyle to the beat of "Jam on It," by Newcleus.

Sir Mix-A-Lot was also doing DJ gigs around the Seattle area, and soon, the two began to cross paths. Then after some words were tossed back and forth, Mix-A-Lot decided to escalate the rivalry. Mix was good friends with Nasty-Nes, so they conspired how to win the war of words. Mix-A-Lot wrote a dis track about Kickin Kevin and Joyce called "Come and Get Some Boys," and he gave it to Nes for his *Fresh Tracks* show on KFOX. Nes played the song on the air one night, and according to Nes, the whole city was buzzing after that. Nes said it was "like watching a Tyson or Manny Pacquiao fight." The song was a very harsh and specific attack on Mike Joyce and Kickin Kevin.

Excerpt:

While you were on the street playing old school beats
I was working 9 to 5 trying to bust concrete
Trying to make a buck to buy a drum machine
While you were at the club flaunting your Guess jeans

Now you're calling me conceited you know who you are
M.J., K.J., the Broadway stars
No I'm not conceited, how much should I repeat it
Don't talk behind my back when you know you can't beat it

DJ M.J., I'm talking to you
Sitting pretty high class in a DJ booth
What did I do to you, what made you run your mouth
A small case of jealousy, ha, no doubt
You're calling me conceited when you wear a bow tie
Patent leather spats and a tear in your eye
I think you're jealous cause of one cold fact
Mix-A-Lot Ray's gonna be on wax
I never stop pushing cause I wanna be better
No valet parking no cashmere sweaters
You're not a real DJ and you're not wax bound
M.J. is just a sucker trying to hold me down
I will be the one to put Seattle on the map
Help any down brother in the city who raps
But people like you and K.J. too
Will always be backstabbers in a DJ booth

M.J., I'm through talking about you
I'm gonna talk about your sidekick, he's weak too
His initials K.J. and his show's alright
He stands behind your back and works the lights all night

Mix remembers writing that song just to see if he could get some publicity for it. The song was classic because it showed the battle approach of early hip hop. "Kickin" Kevin Jones actually looks back on the song with amusement rather than anger. To have someone as big as Mix-A-Lot attack him on the radio was a type of validation. It placed Jones and DJ Mike Joyce on the unofficial list of movers and shakers in the Seattle music scene.

ROTARY BOYS' CLUB MEETING

In June 1984, *The Rocket* ran a piece about KFOX's *Fresh Tracks*. DJ Nasty-Nes had gained a large audience by playing rap mixed with R&B music every Sunday night. "Probably the best two hours of commercial radio in the Seattle area," the write-up began. It went on to say, "Recent segments debuted the music from the movie *Beat Street* including hot hits by Grandmaster Melle Mel and the Soul Sonic Force." One of the "slick" promos that Emerald Street Boys recorded for the show was also mentioned.

Sheila Locke had stopped working as a radio DJ back in 1980, when she and other dissatisfied KYAC staff walked off the job. She explored acting and theater for a while, but her love was always spinning records and DJing at parties. She remained good friends with Nasty-Nes, and they would attend various gigs together.

Nasty-Nes and Sheila Locke went to a Rotary Boys' Club event one evening at Nineteenth Avenue and Spruce Street in order to see Sir Mix-A-Lot perform. Locke and Nes arrived and walked through the crowd. Nes remembers feeling out of place because he and Sheila were the only Asian people there. Giving the moment some context in *Emerald Street*, Dr. Abe summed it up like this: "As it turned out, this moment would be a watershed moment in the evolution of early Seattle hip hop."

Since Nasty-Nes was a famous local DJ at KFOX, Mix-A-Lot really put effort into impressing him, even mixing in an early version of "Square Dance Rap." Mix-A-Lot remembers that a girlfriend was with him on the stage, and she reminded Mix how important it was that he do his best. Finally, after a long set, Locke and Nes approached the stage and were able to speak to Mix. They exchanged information and chatted for a minute. After seeing Mix perform at the event, Sheila and Nes were both very impressed.

Nes and Mix-A-Lot got together soon afterward. Mix-A-Lot had a bunch of songs already recorded, so he passed a tape to Nes. From that

Rotary Boys' Club at Nineteenth Avenue and Spruce Street. *Photograph courtesy of the Seattle Municipal Archives.*

point forward, Nasty-Nes would play Mix-A-Lot songs on his KFOX show *Fresh Tracks*.

Nes remembered the lead-up to the meeting in an interview with Glen Boyd about a year later in *The Rocket*. "[Mix-A-Lot] would be DJing for Jam Delight, while I'd be doing Emerald Street Boys," said Nes. "Rumors started flying about a battle. One night I came to see him, and everyone thought that was gonna be it."

According to Nasty-Nes, one of the earliest Mix-A-Lot tracks he played on air was a demo version of "Let's G." Just like Locke had let a young Nes visit her in the radio booth at KYAC, Nes brought Mix-A-Lot to hang out with him at KFOX. Mix remembers that KFOX station manager Steve Mitchell was mad at Nes for playing the Mix-A-Lot song. "Yeah, I was in the other room while Nes was getting cussed out," says Mix-A-Lot.

Nasty-Nes was amazed at the phone calls he would get whenever he played Sir Mix-A-Lot on his KFOX show. Callers would ask, "Who is this?" and "Where can I get this?" The "7 Rainier" track was just one in a long string of hits that Mix-A-Lot funneled to Nasty-Nes, who then played them on *Fresh Tracks*. Simultaneously, Mix-A-Lot was performing at Boys and Girls Clubs on weekends and sneaking "7 Rainier," along with other songs, into his club sets. People loved it. Mix-A-Lot could gauge the success of his own songs at a party by mixing them in with national rap hits. "7 Rainier" was the one of the first tracks to really go viral for him.

"RHYME ONE TIME"

Jam Delight continued to be a huge force in the Seattle rap scene. There was an article about Jam Delight in the July 20, 1983 issue of *The Facts*. "The original rappers who created the entire rap scene in Seattle are now returning to the Pacific Northwest in an awesome redemption quest to regain recognition as the greatest rappers Seattle has ever encountered," it claimed. The article identified Jam Delight as "two devastating masterminds known as Gary Jam and Big Boss Cross."

By 1984, Sir Mix-A-Lot had stopped spinning records for Jam Delight, and so the group was looking for a DJ. They found one in the most unlikely place. Kerry "Scratch Master K" Hodge moved from Los Angeles to Seattle, and he got a job as the line manager in the kitchen at the Seattle waterfront Old Spaghetti Factory restaurant. In California, Hodge had messed around with breakdancing and tagging, choosing the nickname "Doctor Hodge." But his real love was turntables and DJing, and when he got to Seattle, he started calling himself "Scratch Master K."

Gary Jam and Big Boss Cross needed some income, so they both applied for work and were hired at the Old Spaghetti Factory to work as dishwashers. Soon, the three young men started talking about rap music, and when Jam Delight found out that Scratch Master K was a DJ, they enlisted him to spin records for their live shows. Scratch Master K lived in Rainier Beach, and Jam Delight lived in West Seattle, but they made it work somehow.

Jam Delight did a show at the University of Washington, according to Scratch Master K. "They told us we could go back and get a copy of the tape, but we never did," Scratch Master K remembers regretfully. He recalls that they did shows around Seattle, including at Lateef's, Empire Plaza and The Spectrum nightclub. According to Scratch Master K, he saw Sir Mix-A-Lot in the crowd during the Spectrum show.

In fact, Scratch Master K didn't just live in Rainier Beach; he lived in the Lakeshore Village Apartments, which was the same complex Sir Mix-A-Lot lived in. Scratch Master K remembers Mix-A-Lot's apartment window very well; he would go tap on the window and swap tapes with Mix-A-Lot. Jam Delight would record raps at Scratch Master's apartment using his Roland TR-606 drum machine, often with disses of Mix-A-Lot on them.

Both Gary Jam and Big Boss spent time recording at Scratch Master K's apartment. Gary Jam did a three-minute solo track that began with the lyrics, "Well, I'm ready and set." It included samples from the Malcolm

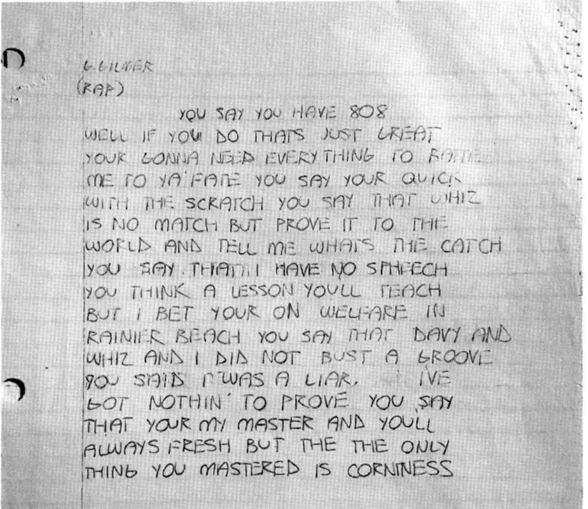

G.GILMER
(RAP)

YOU SAY YOU HAVE 808
WELL IF YOU DO THATS JUST GREAT
YOUR GONNA NEED EVERYTHING TO BAIT
ME TO YA'FATE YOU SAY YOUR QUICK
WITH THE SCRATCH YOU SAY THAT WHIZ
IS NO MATCH BUT PROVE IT TO THE
WORLD AND TELL ME WHATS THE CATCH
YOU SAY THAT I HAVE NO SPEECH
YOU THINK A LESSON YOU'LL TEACH
BUT I BET YOUR ON WELFARE IN
RAINIER BEACH YOU SAY THAT DAVY AND
WHIZ AND I DID NOT BUST A GROOVE
YOU SAID I WAS A LIAR, IVE
GOT NOTHIN' TO PROVE YOU SAY
THAT YOUR MY MASTER AND YOU'LL
ALWAYS FRESH BUT THE THE ONLY
THING YOU MASTERED IS CORNINESS

Left: Handwritten lyrics by Gary Jam. *Lyrics courtesy of Kerry Hodge, photograph by author.*

Below: Kerry "Scratch Master K" Hodge. *Photograph courtesy of Kerry Hodge.*

McClaren song "Dy'a Like Scratchin?" One solo track by Big Boss started out with the line "Come to the party." It ran over seven minutes and featured verse after verse from Big Boss, set to scratches from "Body Work," by Hot Streak. A third track featured both rappers as Jam Delight and started out with the question "Can I cut a rhyme?"

Above: Airbrushed Jam Delight T-shirt. *Shirt courtesy of Kerry Hodge, photograph by author.*

Opposite: "Rhyme One Time." © *1984 TLP Records, scan by author.*

There was a specific Mix-A-Lot song called "She Loves Me," which led to a rivalry. According to Scratch Master K, "She Loves Me" mentioned Gary Jam, and Jam Delight made some songs dissing Mix. Mix quickly recorded a clapback response tape, and this beef may have been the origin of another famous Mix-A-Lot song, "Destroy Gary Jam."

Big Boss Cross and Gary Jam decided they wanted to record a rap onto a record, so one day, they went to visit The Lord's Place Records, which was located right behind Garfield High School. The Lord's Place, or TLP, was a small record store that sold gospel and religious music and also had a small recording studio in the building. TLP was run by Douglas T. Green and T.C. Jenkins. The two of them collaborated on several TLP gospel releases, including Twylla, Tramble & Tramble and Frederick III. Green had also played bass in the Total Experience Gospel Choir, a famous Seattle music group.

Jam Delight asked Green if he could record a hip hop track for them, but he told them that TLP was for religious music only. Green recalls telling them that if they could write a religious rap, he would consider it. So, Jam Delight went home and wrote lyrics for a track about the Christian faith. When it came time to record, instead of using the name Jam Delight, they went by RGS, which stood for "Rhyming Gospel Sensations." Green and Jenkins were producers on the track.

Excerpt:

Another Jamboree, now He's your choice
But let the Lord be the strength of every joist
You can stand tall with a good man's pride
Because it always feels good to be sanctified
Make a good motion beyond good will
And when it's time to be blessed this will fulfill
Be on the path of love and for the cause of grace
Leading straight to the kingdom of the Lord's embrace
We are the subject of a fateful quest
And choose to walk a journey that the angels blessed

You're in the mirror concentrating on your pretty hair
Never thinking about the Man who put it there
You eat your dinner with a real clean attitude
But ain't never took the time to bless your food
Before the eyes of the Lord we will all appear
So let our love for the Lord be given sincere
We'll get down and radiate the pride
And ask the Lord for the strength he will provide

© 1984 Rhyming Gospel Sensations

Green liked the song and decided to release it on seven-inch vinyl, with the same song appearing on both sides. He had the records pressed in Louisiana and then distributed them in Seattle. Green hosted a gospel radio show on KNHC every Sunday, and according to Green, he brought the record to the station and played the song. Right away, he got a very negative response from listeners. They said he was blaspheming by putting the Lord in a rap song.

But Green realized the power of this new art form. He recalls telling the detractors that hip hop was here to stay and that they had better get used to it. Similar to SNECO, he also realized that rap was a new way to spread positive messages in the community.

Jam Delight finally stopped performing for several reasons. Big Boss Cross was getting into street life and the anonymity that went along with it. He later passed away in an automobile accident in 2016. Meanwhile, Gary Jam was pursuing R&B instead of rap. After the group disbanded, Scratch Master K didn't know what to do next, so he kept doing hip hop with his cousin Tommy Walker, also known as "Kool Tee." They went by the name Jam Delight Posse, keeping the name alive.

COSMIC LEGION CREW

Terrence "Maharaji" Matthews was a young man in San Diego when "Rapper's Delight" hit. Shortly after that, Matthews moved to Bremerton and entered high school. Due to his love of b-boying, he soon came together with The Dominoes breakdancing crew. Matthews was known as "Tron" in dance circles. He recalls attending a breakdancing contest in Bellevue that was hosted by Nasty-Nes and Sir Mix-A-Lot. At one point, after the dance portion of the event, everyone ran to the stage to see Mix-A-Lot perform. When Matthews felt the crowd's response to the mixing and rapping, he decided to go home and write his first rap. Sure enough, he went home, listened to the instrumental beat of "5 Minutes of Funk," by Whodini, and wrote a rhyme.

Soon, Matthews teamed up with a rap crew called The Enforcers. They included Derek "Desert Sheik" Hudson, Andre Cole, James "Porno Poet" Sutter and a young woman named "Fantasia." Around this time, Matthews renamed himself "Fresh T." The group recorded a few songs, including "Sands of Time," "Emerald City Freaks," "Systematic" and "Silly Little Girl." They sent tapes to Nasty-Nes at KFOX.

Matthews and Andre Cole were sitting at a bus stop downtown, eating some beef jerky and drinking sodas. They had a boombox tuned to KFOX, and suddenly, they heard DJ Nasty-Nes introducing their song "Systematic." It was amazing, and they celebrated. All of Matthews's friends called his house to congratulate him. This was fine—until the calls went into the night. His dad made a strict rule: no calls after 10:00 p.m., please.

One of the Enforcers, Desert Sheik, moved to Florida, so the remaining three members drifted apart. Matthews tried to get Mix-A-Lot's attention but was not having much luck. One day, Matthews was watching *Lifestyles of the Rich and Famous* on TV when he saw a piece about a wealthy Maharaja. He decided to change his rap name from Fresh T. to "Maharaji."

After hearing the local buzz, Mix-A-Lot became interested in Maharaji's work. One day, Maharaji got a call from Nasty-Nes, inviting him to a meeting with Mix-A-Lot. Mix and Maharaji became friends and would hang out at Mix-A-Lot's Rainier Beach apartment. Later, Maharaji was selected as a Northwest artist to watch in *The Rocket*. He had a hit around this time titled "Seward Park."

Excerpt:

If you're searching for a way to reach your peak
Come to Seward Park with the pretty little freaks
Lay in the grass, let the sun hit your face
Drink cherry coolers while you listen to my bass

I'm Maharaji baby, you know who I am
Come give in to the Seward Park jam
I see you on the sidewalk with your long silky hair
Eyes are light green with your skin complexion fair
Bermuda shorts and those tight, tight jeans
All the guys should name you the Seward Park queen
Hot, hot fun in Seward Park, oh girl
You know I want to get into your world

You delicious dirty girl with all your freaky friends
I see your golden face on the hot weekends
Walking your dogs or playing your box
Beads in your hair with your polka-dotted socks
Make no mistake by staying at home

Come dial a freak on the telephone
So how would you like it if I went and hopped a ferry
I'll leave my phone number, you can even call me Terry
I think of Seward Park on a hot summer day
Come take a deep breath the Cosmic Legion way

There was a long roll-call at the end of "Seward Park." The list included Monica, Sir Mix-A-Lot, Cashay, Jazzy D, The Wicked Angel, Nasty-Nes, Spicy Shannon, Phantom of the Scratch, Desert Sheik and Lawanda.

Eventually, a new group banded together called Cosmic Legion Crew. (The Cosmic Legion Crew are not related to the Cosmic Crew, which was

(*Clockwise from the top*) Anthony "Sir Mix-A-Lot" Ray, Terrence "Maharaji" Matthews, Larry "The White Guy" Serrin, Ron "Attitude Adjuster" Brooks and Stephen "Kid Sensation" Spence. *Photograph courtesy of Karen Moskowitz.*

composed of Sir Slam, Mellow Mike and Sir Skyy.) The Cosmic Legion Crew included Sir Mix-A-Lot, Nasty-Nes, Maharaji, Bart "Phantom of the Scratch" Staeger and Jazzy D from Silver Chain Gang. Jazzy D had been rapping solo for a while, and he joined Cosmic Legion using his new name Funky Fresh Jazz.

Cosmic Legion Crew also included a young woman named Penny who rapped using the name "The Wicked Angel." Thanks to her connection with Sir Mix-A-Lot, she even had a couple of solo songs played on KFOX. Earlier women in Seattle rap, like Emerald Street Girls, Nasty Girls, The Groovy Gangster Girls and The Backbreakers, had performed live but had not recorded any raps onto tapes.

Sir Mix-A-Lot was the producer for The Wicked Angel's songs, and his voice can be heard on her tracks. Her lyrics explained how she used her sexy style and makeup to get flattering attention. "My Lipstick" was a perfect example of this technique.

Excerpt:

You rarely see a freak with lips so moist
But my lips are an exceptional choice
If I blow you a kiss, or whisper in your ear
It's a guarantee baby there's nothing to fear
Sit down relax, listen to what I have to say
You might think you want to leave, but something tells me you'll stay
Ah, kiss me baby, I can taste you from there
Come a little closer baby if you dare
I see you chose plum but then you changed to cherry
Let me tell you homeboy, my lipstick varies
Every last color has a different hue
I'll wear any freaky color baby just for you
I have proved myself to you with hot sexy cherry
It's obvious this ain't Little House on the Prairie

© 1984 The Wicked Angel

Another radio song by The Wicked Angel was "Are You Voluptuous?" This one had a short verse by Mix-A-Lot in the song. Wicked Angel bragged that the two of them can't be defeated. She also launched multiple challenges at other "lady MCs."

Excerpt:

The Wicked Angel, the lady MC
You other female rappers can't hang with me
Because the Wicked Angel's here to rock the house
To show you lady MCs what hip hop is all about
Now before I get started I'd like to say
You other DJs can't compete with Mix-A-Lot Ray
You talk behind his back, you say he's weak
But with the Wicked Angel by his side he can't be beat

It's The Wicked Angel down by law with Mix-A-Lot
I'm sitting here right by his side bumping the box
I'm a fresh female rapper I'm new on the scene
I don't advertise my sex life, I don't rap obscene
I'm not conceited or a flirt that's just not me
Just me and Mix-A-Lot kick back and rock space beats
You other homegirls call Sir Mix-A-Lot and say you can rap
You hang out in his cars and try to sit in his lap

© *1984 The Wicked Angel*

While Mix-A-Lot remembers that there may be others, these two tracks were the first known rap songs ever recorded by a woman in Seattle. Because The Wicked Angel was the first, her rap legacy cannot be underestimated.

"The Wicked Angel." *Photograph courtesy of Keith Brofsky.*

In 1985 Glen Boyd interviewed Nasty-Nes, and they discussed Cosmic Legion Crew. "We've got a fifteen-year-old white rapper and scratcher Phantom of the Scratch, who is really quick," said Nes. "Then there's the Maharaji, whose hit 'Seward Park' has been a hit on the request lines, and another guy called Jazzy D." Nasty-Nes concluded the piece by talking about future plans for the group: "We'll go to all the high schools, even the white schools, with a thirty-minute show to expose them to hip hop."

RECORD STORES

As the '80s progressed, there were more stores in Seattle where DJs could shop for new rap records. Dirt Cheap was still a favorite among early hip hoppers. In 1981, writer Ray Gastil gave a rundown in *The Seattle Sun* of a few popular local record stores. "Both Uniwax records on Broadway and Platters on Lake City Way have a good selection of singles in funk and newer wave rap," he observed. Gastil then pointed out that the chain stores had less selection: "Musicland downtown and other large record stores have the Sugar Hill and Frankie Smith basics."

By 1984, according to *The Rocket*, the popular local shop Little Record Mart was open only four days a week. "Ineta Chambliss has kept her small Black music shop on Madison healthy for 12 years now," began the *Rocket* article. Chambliss explained that she wasn't really an expert. "The only thing I knew about records was buying them and playing them," she joked. Chambliss was apprehensive about selling hip hop music: "Actually I could do without some of these new rap things. But I stock them!" She enjoyed the company of her cat Toby, and generally, there was no music playing in the store. This was odd for some shoppers, but Chambliss enjoyed the quiet.

Like many of his peers, Baron Von Scratch loved record collecting and made it a point to learn all the spots downtown where he could buy albums. Most people went to Musicland on Third Avenue, and Tower Records was also a big seller of vinyl. But then Baron learned that Woolworth had a small but decent record section that had cheaper prices than either Musicland or Tower, so he would often stock up at Woolworth.

After high school, Tony Benton of Teleclere got a job at the Seattle Music Menu record store. He remembers having an early interest in rap music. By 1983, Benton was the manager, and he even set up an entire display rack of all the rap records in their inventory. According to Benton, some customers would eagerly ask if he had any rap, while others believed that it wasn't "real" music.

Penny Lane Records was another spot for early shoppers. Glen Boyd from *The Rocket* managed the Lakewood Penny Lane branch from 1980 to 1984. He was one of the very early vendors of rap in the area. Thanks to Glen's management, the Lakewood location was mentioned by writer Karl Kotas in the March 1982 edition of *The Rocket* as "the best place to pick up rap and funk records these days." Kotas continued, "They've got huge selection and three turntables where you can listen to any new album or 12-inch single."

"Shockmaster" Glen Boyd (*left*) and Nestor "DJ Nasty-Nes" Rodriguez (*right*). *Photograph courtesy of Frank Harlan.*

In a 2009 blog post, Boyd remembered those early days fondly. "After placing a phone call to a New York based rap distributor called Tape King, we ordered our first batch of about one hundred twelve-inch singles," wrote Boyd. Grandmaster Flash and Treacherous Three were two of the titles he ordered. Even though it was a large order, "We sold out in less than a day," Boyd marveled.

Boyd says he will never forget when Harold "DJ Whiz Kid" McGuire did an in-store performance and blew everyone away with his turntable skills. Whiz Kid already had a huge hit called "Play That Beat" on Tommy Boy Records in New York, and he had recently moved to Washington State. Whiz Kid was a real local celebrity as far as hip hop was concerned.

In 1984, Boyd moved to the Music Menu on Twenty-Third and Rainier Avenues, becoming the manager after Tony Benton left the position. Local hip hop artists and DJs would bring their tapes for Boyd to sell on consignment, and he was very proud of his rap selection on the store shelves. "Whether it was Kurtis Blow or The Furious Five in New York, or Trouble Funk in D.C., or World Class Wrecking Crew in LA, [Music Menu] brought it from all around the country and planted it right here in the hood in Seattle," remembered Boyd in a 2011 interview.

Boyd watched, and as the trends in music continued to change, he became more and more interested in local rap. He carried tapes by Big Boss Cross and Sir Mix-A-Lot. Music Menu was an all-around popular hangout. According to Boyd, Gary Jam from Jam Delight worked briefly at Music Menu as a retail clerk.

Boyd became a fixture for the rap-buying public in Seattle, and his knowledge of the genre was encyclopedic. This led to him getting his own radio show in 1987 on KCMU 90.3 called *Shock Frequency*. During his second show, he took a call from Robert Newman from *The Rocket*, and Newman gave Boyd the nickname "Shockmaster." In 1993, a professional wrestler also used the name "Shockmaster," but according to Boyd, this was just a funny coincidence.

1985

FREEZE MCs

Greg "Colonel G" Steen went to Washington Middle School and then attended Roosevelt High School. He remembers that he was a freshman at Roosevelt when Sir Mix-A-Lot was a senior. Steen started hanging out with the Silver Chain Gang, and rapper Sir Wes became a bit of a mentor, helping him create a persona. Steen's first nickname was "Kid Camelot," and he loved reciting lyrics from his favorite rapper, Kangol Kid, from the popular New York group UTFO. Part of developing an image was choosing a good stage name, and Sir Wes helped Kid Camelot come up with a new one: "Colonel G." The alias sounded hard and authoritative, and it stuck.

One day, Sir Wes introduced Colonel G to Frostmaster Chill. Colonel G and Frostmaster got along very well, and they both started hanging out at Frostmaster's grandmother's house, making music in the basement studio. When Kings of Cuts broke up, Daddy D was looking for a new crew. Daddy D had a reputation for being a spitter and a battle rapper, and he joined up with Colonel G and Frostmaster. With the addition of Daddy D, their new supergroup was called Freeze MCs, or alternatively, but less often, Ice MCs. Even though Frostmaster was still friends with Sir Lover the MC, Sir Lover did not join Freeze MCs.

Freeze MCs established themselves as a battle crew. They twice battled Emerald Street Boys, according to Frostmaster Chill. The first time was at

(*Left to right*) Michael "Mellow Mike" Thomas, David "Daddy D" Blanchard and Greg "Colonel G" Steen. *Photograph courtesy of David Blanchard.*

Club Broadway, and Freeze MCs were declared the winners. Then there was a battle at the Encore nightclub, and Emerald Street Boys took the crown at that one.

The group added two female rappers, Dawyne "Dangerous D" Boykins and Lisa "Luscious Lee." According to Colonel G, both Dangerous D and Luscious Lee were official members of Freeze MCs. He remembers that they both performed with the group at a notable Club Broadway show. At this time, there were still very few women MCs beyond Emerald Street Girls and The Wicked Angel.

Colonel G remembers writing verses and then going over to Kevin Gardner's studio on Graham Street. They would pay Gardner a little cash, and he would record them over a beat. The group was very motivated, and Colonel G actually mailed demo tapes to Sugar Hill Records in New York, hoping for a contract deal. Some Freeze MCs songs were "Real NY Style,"

"Toss It Up" and "It's Time to Break." A song called "King of the Hill" got radio airplay, according to *The Rocket*. Daddy D remembers Frostmaster impeccably scratching the chorus for "King of the Hill."

Frostmaster continued his journey to excel at DJing. He went to Club Broadway and listened to Mike Joyce's sets. Joyce was always in sync, and his mixes were spot-on. Once, Frostmaster climbed up to the DJ booth at Club Broadway, which was shaped like a giant jukebox. Mike Joyce was on the wheels of steel. They chatted about mixing, and then Joyce told him, "You better listen. I'm only gonna tell you this once." As Frostmaster recalls, Mike Joyce explained how to measure the beats per minute (BPM) of each record, using a stopwatch and writing down the numbers. Once Joyce knew the BPM of a song, he would write it on the jacket so he could match it with other songs of the same BPM. Frostmaster soaked up every detail.

Frostmaster received another key bit of advice from DJ Sergio Lacour. Lacour was one of the better DJs around, and he provided Chill with the other secret technique aside from BPM. The BPM trick worked on songs with drum machine beats, but there were many songs with live drummers. If you were mixing a live drummer song with a drum machine song, the mix would occasionally drop out of sync. But Lacour had a trick to match these unique songs that didn't exactly match up.

DJ Sergio Lacour showed Frostmaster by cueing up a record, and then he got a second song matched to the first. But as the records played, Lacour used his finger to speed up and slow down the second record at just the right times. This caused the beat to remain matched, but it took finesse. Lacour had to actually push or pull the record gently while it was spinning. Frostmaster put the advice of Joyce and Lacour together to become the best DJ he could.

Frostmaster Chill and Sergio Lacour teamed up to battle other crews as a duo. According to Lacour, it was a good match because they each had different assets. Frostmaster had the basement studio with all the gear and loudspeakers, while Lacour had all the records from his KNHC radio work and his personal collection as a party DJ. Sergio Lacour recalls that he and Frostmaster were once invited to perform at the Nathan Hale cafeteria during lunchtime, which was a wild success.

As Freeze MCs broke up, Daddy D and Colonel G gravitated toward a new group that was coming together called Creative Choice. Frostmaster left Freeze MCs but did not join Creative Choice, and there was some beef after the separation. Frostmaster began working individually with a number of rappers, including Sir Sweet and Dr. Nasty. He also met a DJ around this time named Bryan Hatfield.

J.O.C.

Bryan "J.O.C." Hatfield grew up in the Rainier Valley, and he remembers meeting Captain Crunch from Emerald Street Boys while they were both young. Many first-generation rappers in Seattle remember "Rapper's Delight" being the first rap song they heard. But according to Hatfield, he was already familiar with rap by the time "Rapper's Delight" became popular, thanks to Fatback Band, Funky 4 + 1 and others. While he was still in elementary school, he got excited about mixing records on his own. In a *Rocket* article, Hatfield recalled that he bought his first DJ mixer at Radio Shack for sixty-nine bucks after hearing DST and Grandmaster Flash.

He would shop for records at Musicland downtown, Orpheum on Broadway or Music Menu on Rainier Avenue. He admits that Orpheum was popular because "they had the weakest security," and young people like himself could slip out of the store hiding a handful of records without getting caught. Tower Records, on the other hand, was less popular among his peers, because security there was very tight to prevent shoplifting. "They attached big rectangular plastic frames around the tapes," remembers Hatfield, which made it impossible to hide a tape in your pocket.

As a young teenager, Hatfield began calling himself Jammin' on Cuts, or "J.O.C." for short. He refined his DJ skills and also evolved into a rapper as well, making him a double threat. J.O.C.'s DJ style was mostly about cutting and scratching, rather than blending two records together. This was because only one of his decks had a pitch control, so he couldn't blend like the club disco DJs. Instead, he became better and better on the scratch and cut.

J.O.C. attended O'Dea High School along with Bobby "MC 3-D" Stills. He remembers writing rhymes together with MC 3-D when they were students together. One day, J.O.C. was introduced to a young bopper and DJ named "Icey J." Soon, they became friends, and Icey J told J.O.C. about a guy he knew named Frostmaster Chill, who was very important in the rap scene.

The two of them were at J.O.C.'s house and decided to call Frostmaster. Frostmaster answered and spoke to Icey J for a few minutes. Then Icey J said, "Hold on, listen to my man J.O.C. on the turntables," and J.O.C. did a scratching routine while Icey J held the phone receiver up to the speaker. Frostmaster was impressed with the telephone audition and invited J.O.C. to come over to see his basement studio. J.O.C. was amazed at the matching clean Technics 1200s and the loudspeaker system. He even noticed that the professional styluses attached to the tone arms were the special DJ type.

J.O.C remembers a solo song he wrote called "Wrist Return" around this time, with producer Kevin Gardner making the beat. J.O.C. did both the scratches and raps for "Wrist Return." There was another song titled "Incorporated with Jazzy T," which was produced by Frostmaster and featured a rap by J.O.C. while Jazzy T beatboxes. Frostmaster also remembers a cut they did during this era called "Graveyard."

Frostmaster and J.O.C. were starting to run with tougher guys, and they were intimidating when they traveled as a posse. J.O.C. had become tall, and he had broad shoulders. Sugar Bear from Emerald Street Boys was spinning records at Encore in Renton. J.O.C. and the crew would go to the door at Encore and let Sugar Bear know that they wanted to get in for free. Sugar Bear had to make it happen if he didn't want a fight at the door. J.O.C. teamed up musically with the slightly older Frostmaster Chill, and they became performing partners for live shows.

Frostmaster and J.O.C. would also go to the Mix-A-Lot shows on Friday nights at the Boys and Girls Club at Nineteenth Avenue and Spruce Street. J.O.C. remembers many fights at that space. He and his friends got into more and more criminal activities, doing "smash and dash" robberies, in which they would simply break a store window and grab what they could. The score could be jewelry, watches or even musical equipment. Some of the electronics were quite expensive, nearly the price of a new car. J.O.C. stopped devoting as much time to music and instead pursued other temptations.

ELP AND IMPACT PRODUCTIONS

Sheila Locke created a production company called ELP to put on live music and dance events. One of ELP's largest parties was called Runnin' with the Night. This dance drew hundreds of young people, and ELP made a nice profit from the event.

Through booking shows for local hip hop artists, Locke met many of the musicians in Seattle. She knew that Emerald Street Boys was the biggest name in town. She decided to get them for the next big ELP show. When the Treacherous Three came to Seattle on Friday, August 10, 1984, Locke had her chance. She booked Emerald Street Boys as the opening act and called the show "Beat Street Breakdown."

On the day of the show, Locke picked the Treacherous Three up at the airport. Then they spent the day together and even had a bopping battle

A flyer for Beat Street Breakdown, August 10, 1984. *Flyer courtesy of Sheila Locke, scan by author.*

between Captain Crunch and Kool Moe Dee. Bopping hadn't died yet; it was still a popular activity. Captain Crunch claims everyone agreed that he was the winner that day.

Treacherous Three performed that night at the Exhibition Hall along with Emerald Street Boys. However, according to Locke, the show was a financial loss, and everyone was unhappy with the meager attendance. Unfortunately, this affected the relationship between ELP and Emerald Street Boys.

At some point after that show, Locke created a new entity for promoting and producing live events, choosing the name Impact Productions. During 1985, Impact Productions promoted a number of shows at Seattle Center in order to grow its brand. Locke ran radio and print advertisements for these DJ-based events.

The Treacherous Three show had created distance between Emerald Street Boys and Locke, but there was another event that further frayed the relationship. It was at a Kitsap County show near Bremerton where the incident occurred. The venue was a giant hotel called The Bayview Inn, and Emerald Street Boys were booked for a show by Impact.

But the three members of Emerald Street Boys got into an argument with each other at the venue. "I wasn't there like I usually was to keep the peace," remembers Steve Sneed (of SNECO), who had stayed home for this particular show. Reco Bembry (also of SNECO) was actually there, and he recalls that the group may have been fighting over which songs to perform. He remembers stepping between Crunch and Bear trying to separate the two.

Sweet J shamefully recalled the fight in a 2023 interview: "We acted a donkey amongst each other." According to Sweet J, that fight may have dissuaded Sheila Locke from working with the group to put out a record. Locke remembers The Bayview Inn notifying her that they were scaling back their involvement with Impact after that show. She had already made plans for a giant pool party there, which she would have to adjust.

But just because she had a bad night at The Bayview Inn, Locke didn't give up her dreams for Impact. In fact, Impact was already acting as a management company for Sir Mix-A-Lot. As she realized the potential of Sir Mix-A-Lot's live shows, she focused her energy on this new partnership. In this way, Sir Mix-A-Lot became more intertwined with Locke's business plans.

Mix was very eager to put out his own music on a record. To facilitate this, Locke decided to form a record label called Nastymix Records. The name Nastymix came from Nasty-Nes and Mix-A-Lot's names being combined. Greg Jones, who managed Arnold's and Lectric Palace video game arcades, was a founding investor in the label. By late 1985, Nastymix was established. Locke rented a small office on Elliott Avenue, near the landmark *Post Intelligencer* newspaper building. Her office was small and nondescript. The building was also used by Diamond Parking company.

LOVE SICK RHYMERS

Ray "Eaze" Valrey was in the eighth grade in 1984, and his family lived near Fifty-First Avenue and Creston Street. His early nickname was "Razzy Ray," and he loved all elements of hip hop. He was into dancing and tagging, but of course, the music was key. An early song that perked his ears was "It's Just Begun," by The Jimmy Castor Bunch. He remembers his mom calling him to the TV room as a kid, because a movie called *Style Wars* was airing on PBS. He also recalls going to movie theaters to see the movie *Flashdance* in 1983 and then *Beat Street* and *Breakin'* in 1984.

Zhonyak "Kid Mix" Love resided near Fifty-Sixth Avenue and Bangor Street. As a kid, Love developed an appreciation for music by watching DJs at house parties and festivals and started going by the name "Playboy Z." Over time, he managed to get turntables and an old mixer, which he stored in his bedroom. One year, he saved up money all summer to buy a Dr. Rhythm drum machine.

Love's mother was not a fan of rap music. "That's not music—that's just noise," she would tell him. So, when his mom was at work, he knew exactly how many hours of free time he had. His bedroom was too small, so Love would bring some cinder blocks into the living room, and then he would place some boards on top of the cinder blocks. Next came the record players, and after that, the mixer. Love would plug in all the RCA cables and turn on all the power buttons, and then he would have a DJ setup right in his own house.

Zhonyak "Kid Mix" Love (*left*) and Ray "Eaze" Valrey (*right*). *Photograph courtesy of Christopher Smith.*

One day, Love invited Valrey over, and it was a day when Love's mom was at work. That meant the turntables were in the living room already. Valrey was amazed as he watched Love scratch a record, and then he tried it himself. But soon, Love told him that they had to move everything before his mom got home, so all the gear had to be carried back to be hidden in Love's bedroom.

They came up with a name, the Freak Force Crew, and started riding the bus from the South End to the University District and back. As taggers, they would bring markers or spray paint and write their tag "Freak Force Crew" anywhere they could. Valrey remembers being on the bus, especially route no. 7, and just scanning block after block, looking for the perfect walls. This, of course, was the same bus route referenced by Sir Mix-A-Lot in "7 Rainier." Valrey also remembers that if the police stopped him for questioning, they would always check his hands for ink stains, which would prove he had been tagging.

Zhonyak Love and Ray Valrey were both hooked and became dedicated and totally obsessed with hip hop culture. Around this time, Ray changed his name from Razzy Ray to "Eaze," and Zhonyak switched his handle from Playboy Z to "Kid Mix." One day, Kid Mix saw a cool mural in a picture book of graffiti with the words "Love Sick Bombers." Kid Mix liked the name but said they should switch it to Love Sick "Rhymers" instead. Eaze agreed, and the group now had a name.

The first song that Love Sick Rhymers ever recorded was rapped by Kid Mix in 1984. It was called "Always Have Something to Do with Females," and it was just over a minute long. A slow, bouncy bassline created drama, while a steady drum arrangement accompanied the rhymes. Kid Mix had to play it live on his Dr. Rhythm drum machine while he rapped.

Excerpt:

As life goes on it never fails
I said I always have something to do with females
Females are wise but some are wiser
Some type of rules just like a supervisor
Some are alright and some okay
I'm gonna tell you a story that happened one day
I was walking down the street with my mind deciding
Up came a girl, we started colliding

She said thanks but what's your name
By the way she spoke I knew I had game
Walked for a while, I must have had action
She's looking pretty hard she's the main attraction
Gave her my number she put it aside
She put it in her pocket she was occupied

But life goes on it never fails
I said I always have something to do with females

© *1984 Love Sick Rhymers*

Even though the song was never officially released at the time, it established the beginnings of LSR as an early force in the Seattle rap game. They made copies of the song for their friends. Soon, the group added a third member,

Lamont "Ace One" Mouton. Ace One knew Kid Mix already, as they lived less than a block from each other.

A year after Kid made "Always Have Something to Do with Females," Ace One recorded a track called "Mic of the Gods." It was also recorded at Kid Mix's house. This was a full four-minute track with a very sparse beat. A fifteen-year-old Ace One dropped multiple brags and punchlines.

Excerpt:

I be burning in hell, I'm wanted dead or alive
Don't even try no slap, I'm the wrong kinda guy
A sucker guy went to try and the lady too
Killed the newlywed sucker, destroyed his crew

I'm a young rapper chillin' at fifteen
Sticks stones break bones, but names don't hurt me
Gimme a break, pull out and take five
When I get loose suckers multiply

I'm a Love Sick Rhymer

You wanna battle you'll just get crushed
It takes fifty bad brothers to bite the dust
You're wack on the mic like Captain Kangaroo
You'll need Pepto Bismol when I'm through with you
On the mic I kick ass the most
You wanna battle? Adios Amigos

© *1985 Love Sick Rhymers*

By 1985, it was clear the group was really coming together and starting to build more complex songs. Eaze remembers people mocking rap as only a bunch of human beatbox sounds, but he knew it was so much more than that. The Love Sick Rhymers' catalogue grew slowly at first, but by the late '80s, they were recording dozens of new tracks each year.

JROD

A local musician named Rodney "JROD" Jones graduated from Chief Sealth High School in 1976. He remembers going to Black Arts West at Thirty-Fourth Avenue and Union Street and seeing musical performances as a kid. The house drummer there was named Quincy, and one day, Jones and his friend Gary were watching him drum. Quincy asked them, "Do you want to try it?" And they eagerly picked up the drumsticks. Jones recalls that they practiced even before they had real drums. "We drummed on boxes and five-gallon bucket lids—no joke," recalls Jones. Then Gary finally got a Ludwig set, and they could play on the real instruments.

When rap began to blossom in the early '80s, Jones paid close attention to this growing street culture and started using the nickname "JROD." In 1985, JROD's mother, Alice White, passed away, and he went through some life changes. He left his job, cashing out his retirement, which he used to found a record label called JROD Recordings. The logo incorporated a turntable into the design. Def Jam already had a Technics brand S-shaped tone arm in their logo, so JROD used a Bang and Olufsen–style straight tone arm for his to make it different. Speaking of Def Jam, he watched the rise of the label, and he was especially impressed by the production of Rick Rubin. Songs like "It's Yours," by T La Rock, and "I Need a Beat," by LL Cool J, sounded very original, remembers Jones. Some of his other early favorites were Run DMC and Trouble Funk.

Donnell "DJ 2Smooth" Jackson. *Photograph courtesy of Rodney Jones.*

JROD had a nephew named Donnell "DJ 2Smooth" Jackson. DJ 2Smooth was very talented and soon accumulated some rappers around him who became an informal crew. JROD recalls that Dwayne Banks and Alfie "Pay Me" Mitchell were two early members.

Then a young MC named Lawrence "Pouchie" Moore caught DJ 2Smooth's ear, and the two became a duo called P-D2. The P was for Pouchie, the D was for Donnell, and there were two of them. Pouchie wrote a couple songs, "Michelle" and "In the Shoes of a Bad Man," and there were talks between JROD and P-D2 about doing a project.

But according to Moore, he didn't like the terms of the deal and decided to walk away from the table, quitting P-D2.

This left P-D2 without an MC, but JROD didn't give up. He attended a program at Art Institute of Seattle and began to mingle with other people who wanted to make a career from video or music. Not long after this, DJ 2Smooth met Bobby "MC 3-D" Stills from Southside Three and West Coast Funk Brigade, and the two rebranded P-D2. The new duo went on to release a number of classic titles on JROD Recordings.

KYLEA

Erika "Kylea" White went to Washington Middle School in Seattle. "There was an elevated platform behind the school," she recalls. On this makeshift stage, students would rank or cap other students with clever insults. It was also the place where pop lockers and breakdancers could practice and show off their dances.

Erika "Kylea" White (*left*) and Jonathan "Wordsayer" Moore (*right*). *Photograph by author.*

White has fond memories of listening to KYAC and describes it as the default background music for gatherings or just daily life. She learned how to make "pause tapes," recording the KYAC broadcasts but omitting the commercials and DJ chatter. She vividly remembers the switchover from KYAC to KFOX in the summer of 1981. One day, her basketball team was in a van coming home from a tournament, and someone put the dial to 1250 AM. She heard a weird howl, and the announcer identified the station's name as KFOX. It was quite a shock, she remembers.

She would go shopping for records with her older siblings at stores like Music Menu or Tower Records. "The first record I bought was Prince, *Dirty Mind*," says White.

In 1983, she entered high school at Garfield and made friends with a classmate named Shelindra. When Run DMC's singles hit that year, she was already in love with the developing rap culture. Her friends gave her several nicknames, "E-Dub" and "E White All Night." She remembers that she would hear about Emerald Street Boys performing, but many of their gigs were at twenty-one-and-older establishments. White also recalls people passing around tapes by Anthony Ray before he chose "Sir Mix-A-Lot" as his name.

When she graduated from Garfield in 1987, rap was exploding. She didn't go into music immediately, but several years later, she decided to pursue hip hop as a career. She chose her middle name "Kylea" as her rap moniker. When asked whether she experienced sexism, White replies, "They never told me that I couldn't do it; they just wanted to battle me to see for themselves if I could."

In 1994, Kylea would go on to cofound famous Seattle record label Jasiri Media Group with Jonathan "Wordsayer" Moore. The two partnered and had a son named Upendo. After a long career as one of the best-known and beloved figures in the Seattle rap scene, Jonathan Moore passed away in 2017.

"DOCUMENTARY BREAK DANCE"

Richard Peterson was a trumpet player who would busk for money in public places around Seattle in the 1980s. He would ask for change but had a sign that read, "No Canadian Coins!" This was a rule he took very seriously. In 1982, he put out *Richard Peterson's First Album* on Seattle's King Tut Records.

The monthly "Lip Service" column in *The Rocket* newspaper became obsessed with Peterson during 1983 and 1984. Every issue, the column signed off with a shout-out to Peterson doing various things in various places. One example from August 1984 read, "Richard Peterson, the Northwest grandmaster of the street, does not have a new album out, but he would like to. Until then he is still stuck on the street."

By 1985, Peterson was ready for album number two, and he called it *The Second Album*. This one was on Tan Records. One track on *The Second Album* featured rap and scratching by Chris "Vitamix" Blanchard, an artist from Portland, Oregon, who had made inroads to Seattle's music scene thanks, in part, to *The Rocket* newspaper.

A local studio producer named Peter Barnes recalls the recording session, since he had spent several years working closely with Peterson. In a 2017 film about Peterson, Barnes remembered how Peterson could perform "the famous T and P stunt," which meant playing trumpet with one hand and simultaneously playing piano with the other.

The Second Album. © 1985 Tan Records, scan by author.

Being in the studio with Vitamix was fun, recalls Barnes, and the memory stands out because there were so few rap artists recording in Seattle at the time.

The song they created was called "Documentary Break Dance," and the sound was eclectic. In some ways, the production resembled Malcolm McLaren's work on songs like "D'ya Like Scratchin" or "Hey DJ," which were very popular at the time. Peterson's "Documentary Break Dance" made use of scratching and various other turntable tricks accompanying the basic piano-based melody. There were references to famous score songwriter and composer William Loose.

Excerpt:

Well, my name is Vitamix now check me out
I'm in Documentary to rock the house
I'm rappin' and scratchin' in a real loose style
Vitamix here to put your face in a smile
Mr. Peterson here feeling the groove
While you listen Vitamix can make you move

R.P.'s my man who's always funky fresh
Fixed it up to rock you the best
With help from William Loose and Vitamix
R.P.'s gonna give you Documentary fix
You can do the Smurf, Jerry Lewis, or the freak
But Documentary march is the one to beat

© 1985 Vitamix

In 1985, Vitamix recorded lots of varied material. He produced a song called "That's the Way Girls Are," which got the attention of local label Cold Rock Records. Cold Rock was run by Brett Carlson and DJ Nasty-Nes. Vitamix negotiated with Cold Rock, which later put out the single in a 1986 deal with Profile Records.

"PIG LATIN" AND "FEEL MY BEAT"

One MC who worked with Sir Mix-A-Lot during 1985 was Craig "Jazzy D" Daniels, also known as Funky Fresh Jazz. He had become part of Cosmic Legion Crew and also wrote a couple of solo songs that were produced by Mix-A-Lot. Mix remembers that Funky Fresh Jazz was a true professional when it came to recording raps.

Many others agree that Funky Fresh Jazz was extremely talented. Keith "Sergio Lacour" Samuels remembers Jazz being articulate and somewhat strait-laced. According to Lacour, Jazz could be moody, meaning that the ups and downs in his personal life could really affect his stage presence. A standout track written and performed by Funky Fresh Jazz was called "Pig Latin."

Excerpt:

Listen up freaks easily impressed
By Pig Latin, fast rappin, all that mess
I'm Funky Fresh, every MC's wish
Is they could make Pig Latin sound as good as this

[Rhyming in Pig Latin]

Is there another? Is there another brother
Please tell me who's the other that's as fly and undercover

You know it's fresh, so give me a hand
Any more stars you think I can't rock, man
You say I can't but you know I can
I'm Funky Fresh Jazz peep this rhyme man
I'm the best in the west, let me tell you something
That fast rap crap really ain't nothing

As you can see the best MC, I'm at a university
Rocking to the funky beat always keep it short and sweet
Never, never, never, never ever
Will I be taken out cause I'm just too clever
To ever be beat, I can't be dominated

Nastymix Records sampler cassette. *Photograph courtesy of Sheila Locke.*

I'm the baddest hip hopper ever created
Funky Fresh Jazz def rocker supreme
I can't be beat as easily as it seems

© 1985 Funky Fresh Jazz

Sir Mix-A-Lot remembers recording Jazz's voice on the microphone and thinking that it already sounded compressed. Usually, this was a step that needed to be done in post-production, but Jazz's recordings barely needed it. Another Funky Fresh Jazz song in 1985 was called "Feel My Beat."

Excerpt:

My beats are hard and I am known
As the supreme def rocker on the microphone
I'm the J to the A double Z-Y-D

There's no MC in Seattle that can hang with me
Because I rhyme to the beat, I'm never off time
Sucker MCs scatter when they hear me rhyme
If you doubted me before, I'm gonna get you sprung
Every lyric is def that leaves my lungs

You can't hang with what I release
I rock the Emerald City and I won't cease
I'm Funky Fresh Jazz, rocking KFOX
And as soon as you record it, I'm rocking your box

On your marks, get set, I'm ready to go
Turn the show and break out about 100 below
But before I start and get ready to play
I would like to introduce my DJ
He's Sir Mix-A-Lot, alias Anthony Ray
You suckers talk head about us every day

I lock 'em in the freezer, I like it that way
Nobody rocks like Jazz and Sir Mix-A-Lot Ray
And the Cosmic beat is on your box
My freshest fresh tracks and it does rock
I write rhymes every night, you know that's right
So please don't bite it cause that's not polite
This b-boy is hard you must admit
On your radio station making serious hits
Get down, unstoppable and also untouchable
You ought to know I got a whole lot more
Hip hop won't stop because I can't quit
Inside the Emerald City, I am the hit

© 1985 Funky Fresh Jazz

Both songs by Funky Fresh Jazz made their way to Impact Productions' head Sheila Locke in late 1985. Locke had recently launched her brand-new record label Nastymix to release music from Sir Mix-A-Lot, and was now considering songs from other local artists. She assembled a demo tape in early 1986 of potential releases for Nastymix. After a long rap career, Craig "Funky Fresh Jazz" Daniels passed away in 2021.

EMERALD STREET BOYS BREAK UP

Eddie "Sugar Bear" Wells and Marline Russell were still a couple in 1984. She remembers going to senior prom with him at Roosevelt. However, after graduation, they broke up, and Bear "took it really hard," according to Russell. "He spent the evening expressing his sorrow to one of my girlfriends at the time and, after leaving her home, got into a really bad accident." She recalls that although the group was still performing, this car crash may have coincided with the group's decline.

In Renton, there was a club called Encore run by Keith Olsen. Sugar Bear had a regular gig there mixing records for dancing. Often, Sugar Bear would cut the records or scratch them to the beat, and he was an expert at playing for a crowd.

Sweet J sometimes accompanied Sugar Bear to Encore, and he helped operate the lights. However, Sweet J would often walk around the club, chatting with friends. As Sweet J recalls, the club's owner Keith Olsen would scold him at the end of the night for leaving the DJ booth. One night in 1985, Sugar Bear invited the other two Emerald Street Boys to the stage, and all three performed live raps in front of the club's crowd. Someone at the club recorded the whole session onto a cassette.

That night, the three of them rapped freestyle rhymes to the delight of the crowd. Sugar Bear warmed up the audience with all the usual calls and responses, such as, "The roof is on fire," to which the audience replied, "We don't need no water." Then he said, "When I say peach, you say pear; when I say Sugar, you say Bear." Everybody there was super hyped and yelled along. Then Bear played the instrumental to "Rockberry Jam," by L.A. Dream Team, while the three Emerald Street Boys rapped live to the crowd.

Excerpt:

R-O-B, Rob is what they call me
But I'm better known as the mellow Sweet J
I'm so devious and mischievous
When I turn a party I like it that way
Confident forever and at a steady pace
Guaranteed to win in any MC race

I tend to dominate cause I'm very strong-willed
Self-reliant, I'm the master in the MC field

Yes, yes, y'all, you don't stop
C'mon fly girls I wanna hit the top

My name is Sugar Bear I wanna say hello
I'm gonna prove one thing before I go
There's room in the house for only one MC
So all you other suckers step back please
I'm the original, unforgettable
To rap against me would be unbearable
It will be terrible, be very careful
If you survive alive it'll be a miracle
Ten out of ten say I rock it the most
And I'm proud to say that I'm from the West Coast
I'm a poet, I show it, and if you don't know it
Listen very close and don't you dare quote it

Eventually, the group broke up. Captain Crunch pulled away from the rap scene, and after going through a low period, he found the church to be his source of stability. He pursued this calling with passion, later earning his doctoral degree from A.L. Hardy Academy of Theology. In a romantic turn worthy of fiction, Bobbie "Luscious Lynn" Solomon from Emerald Street Girls and Dr. Croone married in 2013.

After Emerald Street Boys disbanded, Sweet J tried his hand at singing and other pursuits. He also decided to get married. Since then, he has successfully continued with music and broadcasting.

Frostmaster Chill remembers DJing a show for Emerald Street Boys right as they were breaking up. This occurred at the Festival Sundiata, which was an annual Black cultural festival in Seattle founded by Terry Morgan. The way Frostmaster remembers it, "Sweet J performed first, singing rather than rapping." Then Captain Crunch and Sugar Bear went onstage next, just the two of them, and did a hip hop performance, while Frostmaster DJed.

Sugar Bear embraced his identity as a club DJ, and he continued to focus on rapping. This led to Bear's inclusion in a 1990s Seattle rap group called Darkset, along with Frostmaster Chill and others. Eddie "Sugar Bear" Wells passed away in 2019.

Emerald Street Boys had been on top for so long, it was hard to imagine a landscape in the city without them. As the members of Emerald Street Boys retreated from public life, Seattle audiences needed a new act to focus on. Ever since "7 Rainier," Sir Mix-A-Lot had been grinding and pushing. As soon as the old kings of Seattle rap retired, Mix-A-Lot picked up the crown and decided it was his time to shine.

"SQUARE DANCE RAP"

Stephen "Kid Sensation" Spence was a young neighborhood kid who lived on South Henderson Street, just a few blocks away from Mix-A-Lot and Baron Von Scratch. The first time Spence heard "Rapper's Delight," he knew he wanted to be involved with this culture. He and his group of b-boy friends called themselves the GQ Crew, and they practiced breaking and bopping. He also hung out with a rap crew called Chilly Most. Spence remembers writing lyrics to match the instrumental version of the popular 1982 song "The Message," changing it slightly into "My Message."

Spence was curious about Mix-A-Lot. In fact, he would come by and tap on Mix-A-Lot's window just to come in and hang out. One day, Mix-A-Lot and a business partner of his named Larry Serrin were discussing Spence's enthusiasm when they decided to give him an official nickname to join the crew. Spence had been DJing a little and had started calling himself "DJ Dangerous," but he needed a new name. They called him "Kid Sensation" because he was so young.

Kid Sensation became a useful person to have around. When Mix-A-Lot previously did solo shows by himself, he had to prop the door open in his hallway and then carry all the gear out to his car, all while hoping that none of it got stolen. It was a very time-consuming process. With Kid Sensation able to help, Mix-A-Lot could just open his window and hand the gear out to Kid Sensation, who would put it in the car that was waiting in the parking lot. It was very efficient, and Kid Sensation was happy to be a part of the posse. They would drive to the Central District, perform and then drive back to Rainier Beach to put all the electronic equipment back into Mix-A-Lot's apartment.

Sir Mix-A-Lot was performing live all around town throughout 1985. There were at least two shows at The Exhibition Hall, a show on August 3 with Nasty-Nes and a show on September 6 for a "Back to School Prep Dance" with Mix-A-Lot and Cosmic Legion Crew. Nes had been playing a goofy new Sir Mix-A-Lot song called "Square Dance Rap" on KFOX *Fresh Tracks*, and it was becoming familiar to many Seattle listeners.

"I Just Love My Beat." © *1985 Nastymix Records, scan by author.*

Mix was invited on an early tour along with Rappin' Duke, Egyptian Lover and others. He wanted to bring Kid Sensation along, so he paid a personal visit to Kid's mother and asked if they could bring him. Kid Sensation remembers the conversation well. Mix-A-Lot and Mrs. Spence sat down, and Mix explained the tour to her. She wasn't really impressed with rap: "Do you mean to tell me that you're going to take my fourteen-year-old son and give him money to do the rapitty-rap thing onstage?" She laughed at the possibility but finally gave her consent to Mix-A-Lot, and Kid was able to join the tour.

After agreeing to a deal with Sir Mix-A-Lot, Sheila Locke hired lawyer Neil Sussman to help draw up a contract. In fact, it was the same Neil Sussman who had DJed the party for On the Boards' fifth anniversary way back in 1982. Sir Mix-A-Lot put together a four-song EP, which contained songs he recorded at his Rainier Beach apartment and at Steve Lawson Studios. The four songs were, "I Just Love My Beat," "Square Dance Rap," "Let's G" and "Mix-A-Lot's Theme."

Sheila Locke remembers driving in Los Angeles and hearing "I Just Love My Beat" on the radio for the first time. She was astonished. They had done it, she thought. But it turned out that "I Just Love My Beat" was soon eclipsed by "Square Dance Rap."

For the vocals of the song "Square Dance Rap," Sir Mix-A-Lot used a similar technique as Little Ray Rapper and The Chipmunks, in terms of speeding up the tape to make a high-pitched Smurf effect on the voice. It lent a humorous quality to the final sound and made it fun to sing along to the lyrics. From "I'm Little Ray Rapper" in 1981 to "Square Dance Rap" in 1985, the high-pitched voice had come full circle in Seattle rap.

Right away, "Square Dance Rap" began to catch on outside of Seattle. Kid Sensation remembers on tours that even just the first few notes of "Square Dance Rap" would immediately send the crowds into a frenzy. Mix-A-Lot and Nasty-Nes did a Seattle Center Exhibition Hall show on January 14, 1986, to celebrate the achievement. Locke's Impact Productions also held a record release party for the EP at Bayview Inn, which had decided to forgive Impact for the Emerald Street Boys show. According to the flyer, the "Square Dance Rap" event was held on January 31. Soon, the record had sold ten thousand copies—and then fifty thousand! And the sales kept growing.

Sir Mix-A-Lot had gone viral, the first rap artist from Seattle to achieve this feat. His instant fame made him an idol—but also a target. As a barrier to all the attention, Mix adopted a slightly villainous persona, like J.R. Ewing from *Dallas*, a popular show in the mid-'80s. Mix even used the slogan "the man you love to hate" when describing himself. But whether you loved Mix or hated him, one thing was clear: as soon as "Square Dance Rap" became a hit, rap music in Seattle graduated to the next level.

BIBLIOGRAPHY

1980

Ford, Sylvester. "Soul Street." *The Facts*, January 17–January 23, 1979, 8.

———. "Soul Street." *The Facts*, August 15–August 22, 1979, 6.

———. "Soul Street." *The Facts*, August 22–August 29, 1979, 6.

KCMU 90.3 FM. "Rap Attack." Seattle, WA. Aired September 1997.

O'Brien, Tom. "Non Peaceful Co-Existence." *The Rocket*, December 1980, 17.

1981

Abe, Daudi. *Emerald Street: A History of Seattle Hip Hop*. Seattle: University of Washington Press, 2020.

Boyd, Glen. "Soul Man." *The Rocket*, December 1987, 13.

Duncan, Don. "Seattle's New Name Is a Gem." *The Seattle Times*, September 17, 1981, B1.

Franklin, Dre. "The Social Sciences Show." YouTube. February 5, 2021. https://www.youtube.com/watch?v=M9wF3yvY1dY.

Gastil, Ray. "The Rappers." *The Seattle Sun*, September 16, 1981, 7.

Monk One. "Red Bull Music Academy." YouTube. August 27, 2017. https://www.youtube.com/watch?v=ielhwYDFymc.

Newman, Robert. "Armory Wrap Up." *The Rocket*, March 1982, 15.

———. “Here’s the Facts, It’s the Rap, Black Radio’s Back.” *The Rocket*, January 1982, 9.
Renton, Johnny. “Lip Service.” *The Rocket*, April 1982, 12.
The Rocket. “All the Way Live.” November 1982, 34.
———. “Boss Cross.” November 1986, 9.
Rubik and E-Dawg. “The Emerald City Beginning.” YouTube. October 28, 2020. https://www.youtube.com/watch?v=ykHZTiCmt6U.
The Seattle Post Intelligencer. “Theater.” What’s Happening. July 3, 1981, D12.
The Seattle Times. “Stage & Screen.” Tempo. July 3, 1981, 18.
Williams, Lonzo. “NWA Stories.” YouTube. January 28, 2021. https://www.youtube.com/watch?v=eyDBjZ2skrU.

1982

Abe, Daudi. *Emerald Street: A History of Seattle Hip Hop*. Seattle: University of Washington Press, 2020.
———. “Going Way Back.” *The Stranger*, August 10, 2006.
Barbara, Hanna, producer. *The Wacky Races*. Episode 14A. Aired 1968.
Base Camp Studios 2. *As Many Weirdos as Possible*, art gallery exhibit, Seattle, WA: April 4–May 11, 2024.
Blecha, Peter. “East Madison/East Union Mardi Gras Festival Debuts in Seattle on August 4, 1952.” HistoryLink.org. November 17, 2019. https://www.historylink.org/File/20908.
Boyd, Glen. “Funk ’83 Overview.” *The Rocket*, January 1984, 19.
The Facts. “Pacific Northwest Black Community Festival Association Presents Entertainment 83.” June 8–June 14, 1983.
———. “What’s Happening Seattle?” July 14–July 20, 1982.
Newman, Robert. “Affection/Defection.” *The Rocket*, September 1983, 25.
———. “Armory Wrap Up.” *The Rocket*, March 1982, 15.
———. “Funk.” *The Rocket*, September 1982, 36.
———. “Telekinetic Teleclere.” *The Rocket*, October 1982, 19.
Pavitt, Bruce. “Sup Pop.” *The Rocket*, April 1983, 30.
———. “Sup Pop.” *The Rocket*, May 1983, 31.
———. “Sup Pop.” *The Rocket*, June 1983, 32.
———. “Sup Pop.” *The Rocket*, October 1983, 31.
———. “Sup Pop.” *The Rocket*, December 1983, 29.
Renton, Johnny. “Lip Service.” *The Rocket*, April 1982, 12.
———. “Lip Service.” *The Rocket*, May 1982, 12.

The Rocket. "May We Suggest." March 1982, 35.

———. "May We Suggest." April 1982, 40.

———. "1982 How Bad Was It?" January 1983, 26.

Rubik and E-Dawg. "The Emerald City Beginning." YouTube. October 28, 2020. https://www.youtube.com/watch?v=ykHZTiCmt6U.

1983

The Facts. "It's Entertainment Live!!" June 22–June 28, 1983.

———. "Sneco's Showbizz." February 8–February 14, 1984.

Gastil, Ray. "The Rappers." *The Seattle Sun*, September 16, 1981, 7.

James, Kelvin. "Emerald Street Boys Will Soon Wrap on Wax." *The Facts*, September 21–September 27, 1983.

Loewen, Kerry. "Seattle." *Trouser Press*, February 1983, 35.

Penn, Roberta. "C.T. and the Record Band." *The Rocket*, June 1985, 31.

The Seattle Post Intelligencer. "Rappin and Poppin with the Emerald Street Boys and Girls." What's Happening. May 27, 1983, 24.

1984

Boyd, Glen. "He Is the Nastiest." *The Rocket*, September 1985, 10.

———. "To The Hip, To the Hop, Ya' Don't Stop: My Introduction to Hip-Hop." BlogCritics.org. December 4, 2009. https://blogcritics.org/to-the-hip-to-the-hop.

Dexter, Gene. "Meet a Seattle Retail Legend." YouTube. April 16, 2011. https://www.youtube.com/watch?v=YYmEeMXmgfU.

The Facts. "Jam Delight." July 20–July 26, 1983.

Feeney, Sheila Anne. "Break Dancing." *The Seattle Times*, February 19, 1984, F1.

Gastil, Ray. "The Rappers." *The Seattle Sun*, September 16, 1981, 7.

KOMO 4. "Summer Break." Seattle, WA. Aired on September 1, 1984.

Kotas, Karl. "Funk." *The Rocket*, March 1982, 31.

Portnow, David, and Novocaine132. "On the Couch: Danny Dee Rock & Nerdy B." YouTube. November 23, 2020. https://www.youtube.com/watch?v=IbAzOWJt8po.

Rainier Avenue Radio. "Night Beat." Seattle, WA. Aired in June 2021.

The Rocket. "May We Suggest." June 1984, 36.

The Roving Rocket Record Reporter. "Specialty Record Stores." *The Rocket*, March 1984, 17.

Toledo, David. "Genius Among Us." *Vibrant Arts Magazine*, November/December 2019, 12.

1985

Boyd, Glen. "The Big Chill." *The Rocket*, March 1986, 9.

Croone, Ryan. "The Cide Show." YouTube, August 18, 2023.

Harder, Kenny, Scott Milam and Todd Pottinger, dirs. *Big City Dick: Richard Peterson's First Movie*. New Ziv Pictures, 2004.

Renton, Johnny. "Lip Service." *The Rocket*, August 1984, 10.

The Rocket. "The Calendar." August 1985, 32.

———. "The Calendar." September 1985, 27.

ABOUT THE AUTHOR

Novocaine132 was born in Seattle and graduated from the University of Washington. He has been a music journalist since the mid-1990s at magazines including *The Flavor*, *The Rocket* and *The Stranger*. Between 2016 and 2021, he directed three short documentary films. From 2020 to 2022, Novocaine132 was the executive producer of four albums for Ever Rap Records in Seattle. His interest in rap music goes back to his first rap cassette by KTEL in 1984, containing memorable hip hop classics like "Electric Kingdom" and "Tour De France." *The Birth of Seattle Rap* is his first book.

Visit us at
www.historypress.com